Macdonald
Educational

The

The author wishes to thank Dr H. Catling,
Director of the British School of
Archaeology at Athens, Professor A.
Snodgrass of Cambridge University,
Professor F. Walbank of Liverpool
University and Mr H. Russell Robinson of
the Tower of London for their advice and
help in checking the manuscript and
illustrations. He would also like to thank
the Greek and Roman Department of the
British Museum for their help and
encouragement.

First published 1977
Reprinted 1977, 1980, 1982
Macdonald & Co (Publishers) Ltd
Maxwell House
Worship Street
London EC2A 2EN

ISBN 0 356 05580 9

Made and printed by
Hazell Watson & Viney Ltd
Aylesbury
Buckinghamshire

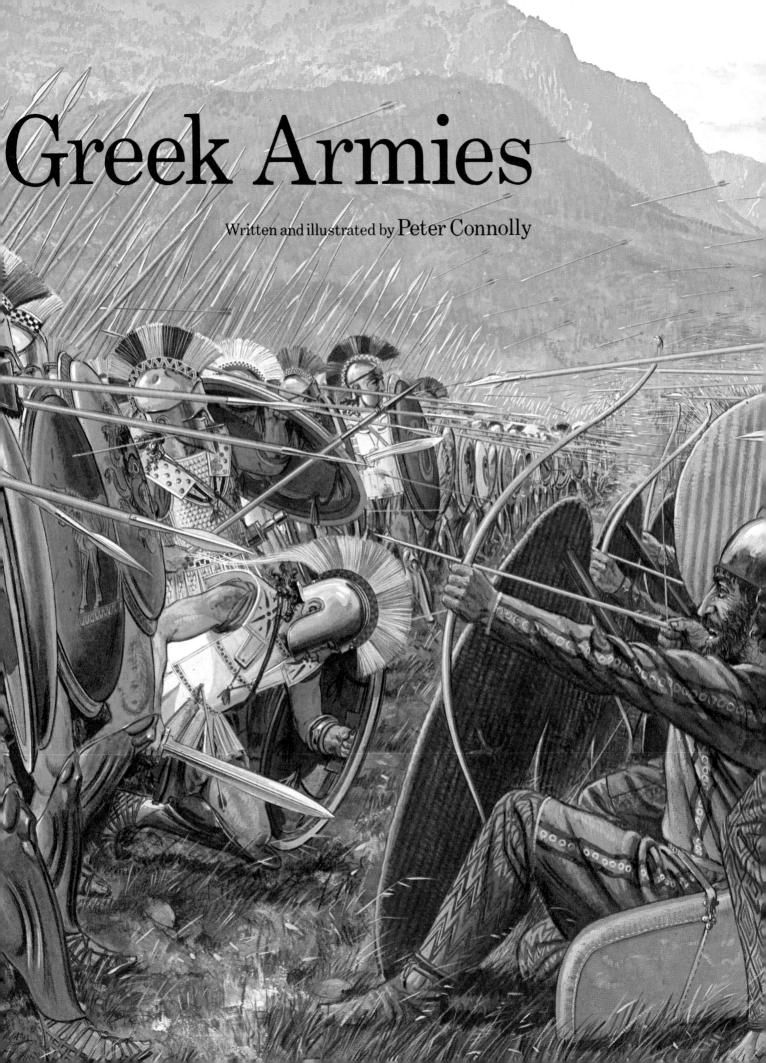

Greek Armies

Written and illustrated by Peter Connolly

The

The military history of Greece goes back over fifteen hundred years, beyond the legendary siege of Troy to a glittering bronze-age civilization. Only a century ago people never dreamed that such a civilization existed. The first part of this book discusses the evidence for the warrior of the time of the Trojan war and tries to relate the archaeological evidence to the descriptions of Homer. The text at the top of each page gives an exciting account of the events based on Homer's writings, whilst the text and illustrations below piece together the fascinating archaeological and literary evidence for the period.

Within a century of the siege of Troy the bronze-age civilization collapsed and Greece disappeared into a dark age. It did not emerge from this until the 8th century BC. The second part of this book deals with the armies of the city states during the 5th century BC when Greece came to military prominence with the defeat of the Persians. It examines the military systems of Athens and Sparta against the background of the Persian wars and later the war between Athens and Sparta. By the 5th century BC Greek armour and military tactics were being adopted by all the civilized people of the western Mediterranean.

The last part follows the rise of Macedon. In the latter part of the 4th century BC Macedon, under its king Philip II, suddenly emerged as a formidable adversary. The other Greek states fell easily to this new power. Philip was assassinated shortly after the conquest of Greece, but his son, Alexander, searching for glory, turned his eyes towards Persia and set out on the greatest campaign of conquest in the history of the world. This part also discusses the advances made in military tactics and technology in the 4th to 3rd centuries BC against the background of Alexander's conquest of the east. The book ends with Alexander's final battle at Hydaspes.

Greek Armies

CONTENTS

The Age of Heroes

During the second half of the 13th century BC a Greek army crossed the Aegean sea and laid siege to the town of Troy on the north-west coast of Turkey. This was the famous siege of Troy. It was the last memorable act of a brilliant civilization that was shortly to collapse and disappear into obscurity. But, like the knights of King Arthur, the heroic deeds of this army lived on in legend. They were immortalized by the blind poet Homer in his two great epic poems —the *Iliad* and *Odyssey*.

Until the end of the last century these poems were treated as myths. It was believed that the Greeks did not emerge from savagery until the 8th century BC. One man, Heinrich Schliemann, believed in the legends. He was not an archaeologist or a scholar. Using the poems as his guide he set out for Turkey and astonished the world by digging up Troy. Since then many sites have been uncovered, proving that a brilliant civilization existed a thousand years before the time of Plato. This civilization began in Crete but later concentrated on mainland Greece. The mainland civilization is known as Mycenaean, after Mycenae, the chief city of Greece at the time.

The Homeric poems bristle with descriptions of warriors and their deeds. During the dark ages that followed the fall of Mycenae these stories were embellished with details from later eras. It was not until they were written down in the 8th century BC that they received their final form.

Excavations carried out over the last century have produced a wealth of archaeological evidence which enables us to begin to build up a picture of the Homeric warrior.

◄ *A Mycenaean war party of the 15th century BC. They have dragged their ship up the beach and are preparing for battle. These are the men who inspired Homer.*

9

The Warrior and his Weapons

The Trojans storm the Greek camp

The Greek soldiers lay asleep with their heads on their shields, their spears, stuck in the ground beside them, casting long shadows. All along the beach their black tarred ships had been dragged clear of the water and propped up on either side. Above them rose the black mass of the turf rampart which surrounded their camp.

Across the fields was a low hill crowned with a massively walled town. This was Troy: the town they had come to capture so long ago. For nine frustrating years they had camped before these walls.

▼ *Paintings of Mycenaean warriors from the palace at Pylos, c. 1200 BC.*

▲ *A heavy-armed chariot warrior, c. 1400 BC. He probably did not carry a shield.*

There was dissent between the generals in the Greek army. Achilles had quarrelled with Agamemnon, the leader of the expedition, over one of the captive women. Achilles, the great warrior, had withdrawn to his hut and refused to allow his men to take any further part in the war. The soldiers were dispirited and talked of sailing home.

When the Trojans learnt that Achilles had withdrawn, they had counter-attacked and driven the Greeks back into their camp. Now, as soon as it was light, they renewed their attack. They charged the rampart in mass and burst into the Greeks' camp.

The Homeric warrior

The warrior described by Homer is a patchwork figure. Although much of his description is true for the 13th century BC, details have been added not only from Homer's own day (8th century BC) but also from earlier periods.

Homer's warrior rides into battle in a chariot. He selects an enemy, gets down and fights on foot in single combat. He is armed with two long throwing spears and a sword. He wears body armour, helmet and leg guards. His shield is large and hangs from a strap around his neck, and can be swung round to protect his back.

Single combat

It would be impossible to fight a battle as a series of single combats as Homer describes. Although no formation as rigid as the phalanx of later times existed, there must have been some battle formation. Traces of this appear vaguely in the *Iliad* in such expressions as "arrayed like a wall," "advancing rank upon rank" and "Achilles, breaker of the line".

The reason for Homer's concentration on single combat is literary—it is far more exciting than the impersonal clash of armies.

Archaeological evidence

Excavations have produced many pictures of warriors, most of whom wear helmets and fabric greaves but no other armour. However, the discovery of a complete suit of armour, shown overleaf, confirms that body armour was in use. There are many representations of the great body shields described by Homer (p.14) and also of chariots, which are discussed on page 16. Most of the archaeological material comes from the high Mycenaean period in the 15th century BC. The main part of this section will therefore deal with this period. The later period (c. 1200) is dealt with on page 22.

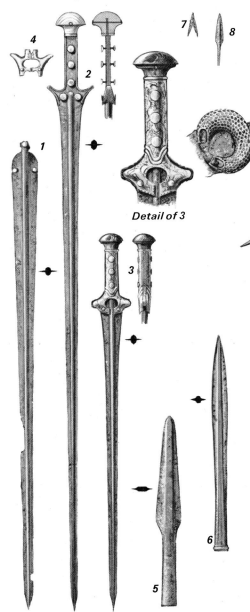

Detail of 3

7. *Dart arrowhead from Pylos.*
8. *Tanged arrowhead from Knossos.*
9. *Sword handle from Mycenae.*
10. *Dagger from near Pylos.*
11. *Short sword from Knossos.*

1. *A round-shouldered sword.*
2. *A horned sword.* **3.** *A cross sword.*
4. *A gold hilt of a horned sword.*
5 *and* **6.** *Two spear heads. All scale 1:6.*
1 *and* **4.** *from Mycenae.*
2, **3**, **5** *and* **6.** *from Knossos in Crete.*

Swords

Many bronze swords have been recovered. They are rapier-like weapons with a strong mid-rib. A round-shouldered type (**1**) was used in the 16th century BC, but this was replaced by two types with stronger handles (**2** and **3**) in the 15th century BC. These long swords soon disappeared, but a short type (see **11** and the Pylos fresco opposite) remained in use until c. 1200 BC. The slashing sword which could sever an arm, described by Homer, is from the later period.

Many short daggers have been found. They are sometimes highly decorated.

Spears

Homer's long throwing spears are probably a confusion between the long spears of the middle Mycenaean period and the javelins of his own day. Spearheads of the type shown left (**6**) are sometimes more than half a metre long.

Arrow heads

Arrow heads in a great variety of shapes have been found. Early in the period the dart type, often made of flint or obsidian, predominates, but later a cast-tanged type appears.

11

Body Armour and Helmets

The Dendra panoply

Most of the warriors described by Homer wear bronze body armour (cuirasses). Until a few years ago it was believed that the poet was describing armour used in his own day. In 1960, at Dendra, not far from Mycenae, a late 15th-century warrior's grave was discovered. This grave contained a complete suit of armour.

This very complex armour consists of two main pieces for the chest (**A**) and back (**B**). These are joined on the left side by a primitive hinge (**C**). There is a bronze loop (**D**) on the right side of the front plate and a similar loop on each shoulder. These fitted into slots in the back plate to join the right side and shoulders. Large shoulder guards (**E-E**) fitted over the cuirass. There were also arm guards (**F-F**) and a deep neck guard (**G**). Three pairs of curved plates (**H-H**) hung from the waist to protect the thighs. All these pieces were made of beaten bronze lined with leather which was turned over the edges of the bronze. Two triangular plates (**J-J**) were found lying on the chest. These were attached to the shoulder guards and gave added protection to the chest.

◀ The Dendra armour as it was discovered in the grave. The neckguard is at the top. Three bronze vessels are at the bottom.
▲ An exploded reconstruction of the armour. **C** shows the inside and outside of the hinge that joined the left side. **X** and **Y** show the method of suspending the front girdle plates.

► *A bronze helmet from Knossos in Crete.*

▼ *A linear-B symbol thought to be for a suit of armour.*

Dendra armour reconstruction

The triangular breast plates and the arm guards were attached to the shoulder guards with cords or leather thongs. The shoulder guard was held to the cuirass by a loop. The neck guard probably had a hole at each side corresponding to the single hole on each shoulder of the cuirass.

The greatest problem is the fixing of the lower plates which have too many holes. The three pairs of holes on the top and bottom of each plate and along the bottom of the cuirass are obviously for loops which joined the pieces together. However unless the loops at the front are slack it is impossible to bend down (see illustration p.8). For this reason the plates had to be suspended on thongs from the larger holes which appear above the pairs on the front plate of the cuirass and on the two upper front girdle plates (see left **X** and **Y**).

In the excavation report it has been suggested that the leather lining did not fold over edges where the metal was doubled back, but in many cases there are clear traces of the lining along these edges. It therefore seems likely that the lining folded over all the edges.

This panoply probably belonged to a chariot warrior. It is far too cumbersome for an infantryman.

Helmets and linen cuirasses

Homer mentions linen cuirasses which would correspond well with the linen greaves shown on so many wall paintings. During the siege of Troy Homer often refers to flashing bronze helmets with horsehair plumes nodding above them. Only one complete helmet from this period has been discovered. It comes from Knossos in Crete. Its date is late 15th century BC. It is composed of a cap with a cast-bronze crest knob and two cheek pieces.

1. *An ivory model of a boars' tusk helmet from Mycenae.*
2. *Pictures of boars' tusk helmets on a silver vase from Mycenae.*
3. *Painting of a late boars' tusk helmet from Pylos, c. 1200 BC.*
4. *Studded fabric helmet or a bronze embossed helmet possibly depicting an invader or foreign mercenary (see p.23), c. 1200 BC from Pylos.*
5. *Examples of pierced boars' tusks from Mycenae.*
6. *Bronze cheek piece from the boars' tusk helmet found in the warrior grave at Dendra.*

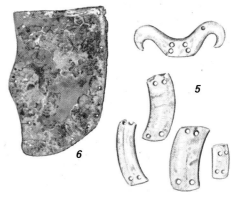

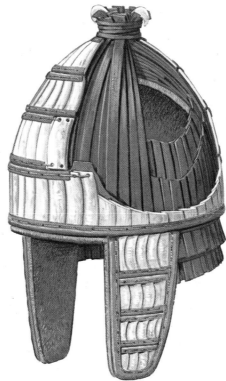

▲ *Reconstruction of a boars' tusk helmet showing felt lining and under-cap made of leather thongs.*

Boars' tusk helmets

In the *Iliad* Homer describes Odysseus putting on a helmet made of boars' tusks —"a helmet wrought of hide, with many a tight stretched thong was it made stiff within". On the outside boars' tusks were "set thick on this side and that". The helmet had a lining of felt. Pierced boars' tusks have been found on many sites including the warrior's grave at Dendra. Paintings and carvings of these helmets are innumerable.

The "tight stretched" thongs if laid fanwise would have made an under-helmet much thicker at the top than at the sides—see illustration. This is the very point at which the helmet needs its greatest strength. An ivory head from Mycenae (1) shows a boars' tusk helmet with two layers of what must be leather thongs hanging down the back to form a flexible neckguard.

Shields, Arm and Leg Guards

Achilles arms for battle

Retreating down the beach the Greeks were forced to fight a last-ditch stand beneath their ships. The warriors stood shield to shield. The archers crouched and shot from between them. The Trojans hurled blazing brands on to the boats trying to fire them. Again and again the Greeks beat them back.

In his desperate plight Agamemnon sent messengers to Achilles begging him to come to his rescue. But in spite of the entreaties of his friends Achilles refused. Finally he agreed to allow his closest friend, Patroclus, dressed in his armour, to go to the aid of

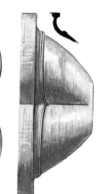

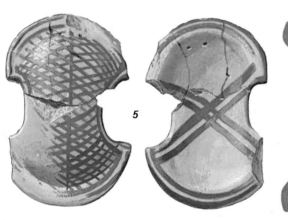

1. The central rib of the lion-hunt dagger from Mycenae. It shows figure-eight and tower shields. Shoulder straps are clearly shown.
2. Ivory model of a figure-eight shield from Kadmeia, Thebes (restored).
3. Painting of a figure-eight shield from Mycenae.
4. Tower shields on a painting from Thera.
5. Clay model of an 8th-century shield with stretchers on the inside.

Body shields

"As Hector walked off, the dark leather rim of his bossed shield tapped him on the ankles and the neck." So Homer describes the great shield of Hector. There are many other references to these giant body shields: Aias' shield is like a city wall; Agamemnon's shield could shelter a man on either side.

The Homeric shield is sometimes described as round. Round shields are very seldom seen in Mycenaean art, but the 12th-century sea peoples and the Greeks of Homer's day used them. However these could never be described as body shields. The poet is probably referring to shields with curved rims, such as the figure-eight type.

The figure-eight shield

The type of shield most commonly shown in Mycenaean art is the figure-eight (1, 2 and 3). This type gradually disappears after 1400 BC but reappears in a modified form in the 8th century (5). It has been argued that this later form is not a real shield at all but an heroic form. There are two objections to this; firstly, primitive artists always draw historical characters in contemporary dress; secondly, the artist who made this clay model of a shield knew exactly what he was making for it obviously represents a wicker shield with stretchers on the inside. If this is a genuine shield then it follows that the figure-eight type existed throughout the Mycenaean and the dark ages.

14

the Greeks. In the guise of the great warrior Achilles, Patroclus managed to drive the Trojans from the camp. But Patroclus was struck down in the midst of the battle and killed by Hector, the Trojan champion.

In anguish and fury Achilles cried out to the gods for vengeance. We are told that Athena heard his cry and brought him a new set of armour. First he fitted his leg guards and then his body armour. Across his shoulder he slung the baldric of his great hide shield. Finally he placed his crested helmet upon his head. He flexed his arms and legs to ensure that his movement was unimpeded then, seizing his spear, he climbed into his chariot and raised the war cry. He charged into the thick of the battle, striking fear into the Trojans, many of whom fell before his mighty spear.

At last he came face to face with Hector. He rushed forward with a roar, and hurled his spear, but the deadly weapon missed its mark and in the confusion of the battle Achilles lost sight of his enemy.

With Achilles in command the Greeks threw the Trojans back to the walls of their town. Here once more Achilles came face to face with Hector. This time Hector lost his nerve, turned his chariot and fled.

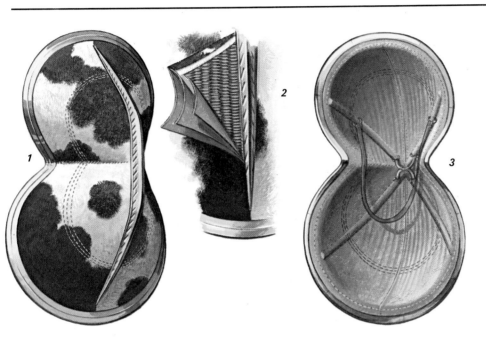

1. *Reconstruction of the outside of a figure-eight shield.*
2. *Cutaway to show wicker core and layers of hide.*
3. *Inside of shield showing cross-stretchers and neck strap.*

Leg and arm guards

Warriors and hunters are often shown wearing what appear to be fabric leg guards wrapped around the lower leg. They are bound at the ankle and just below the knee. A fragmentary bronze greave was found in the warrior grave at Dendra. In the 12th century the egg-shaped central-European type appeared in Greece. This type remained in use down to the 8th century (see p.23). The warrior grave at Dendra has also produced what seems to be a lower arm guard.

The construction of the shield

The shields described in the *Iliad* are made of several layers of hide. These were probably stuck together and stitched on to a wicker frame. This stitching is shown clearly on paintings from Knossos. These shields have a long boss probably made of bronze or rawhide and a rim of similar material. The sides were pinched in so much that the warrior literally got inside his shield (see **1** left). One of Homer's shields has two "rods". These are obviously stretchers. These rods were fitted on the inside and would have been necessary to keep the shield in shape.

Tower shields

Large curved rectangular shields are sometimes shown on paintings. These are known as "tower shields". This type disappears before 1400 BC. Both figure-eight and tower shields hung from a shoulder strap and could be swung round on to the back when running away. They probably also had a central handgrip.

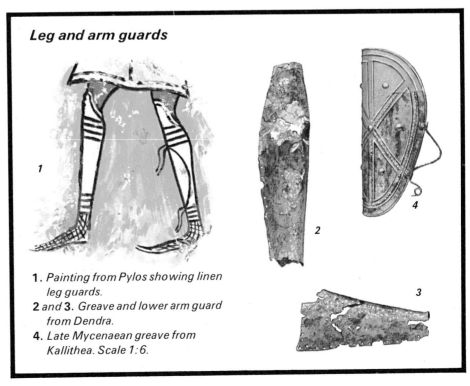

Leg and arm guards

1. *Painting from Pylos showing linen leg guards.*
2. and 3. *Greave and lower arm guard from Dendra.*
4. *Late Mycenaean greave from Kallithea. Scale 1:6.*

Chariots

Achilles and Hector in single combat

When Achilles' driver saw Hector fleeing he lashed his horses and gave chase. After a great race around the walls of the town Hector finally turned and faced his pursuer. Achilles charged, hurling his great spear. But the Trojan ducked and the spear passed harmlessly over him.

Now Hector sprung up and his spear hurtled towards Achilles. The spear struck Achilles' shield but failed to pierce it. Hector drew his sword and rushed in to close quarters. Little did he realize that Achilles, either by the help of the gods or in the con-

▲ An ivory casket from Cyprus.

▼ Chariot and horse paintings.
1 and **2.** From Tiryns. **3.** From Pylos.
4. From Hagia Triada, Crete.

Homer's chariots

In the *Iliad* chariots are used not for massed charges but for carrying a warrior to the front line. Here he alights and fights on foot. It is unbelievable that chariots were used in this way such a short time after the great chariot battle between the Hittites and Egyptians at Kadesh (c. 1300).

A military inventory found in the armoury at Knossos in Crete lists no less than 1,000 pairs of chariot wheels and 340 chariot bodies. These can hardly have been a taxi service for the nobility.

The archaeological evidence

Although there are many representations of chariots from the bronze age no recognizable chariot parts have been found. The representations are too stylized to give a clear impression. They do however show two-horse chariots, four-spoked wheels, central yoke poles and horses with bunched manes. A carved ivory casket from Cyprus (see above) shows a chariot from the Trojan war period being drawn by horses wearing blankets and blinkers. However it has strong Egyptian influences.

A painted coffin from Hagia Triada in Crete (see left) suggests that chariots were hide covered. The horses on this painting are crested and possibly wear faceguards and blinkers.

▲ A linear-B chariot symbol.

16

fusion of the combat, had regained his spear. This time Achilles' aim did not fail and the deadly bronze-pointed spear plunged deep into Hector's throat. With a clatter of armour the Trojan champion fell to the ground. Achilles rushed up and stood towering over his fallen foe. As he lay dying, Hector begged Achilles not to throw his body to the dogs. Scornfully, the Greek withdrew his spear and stripped Hector's body of its armour.

Then other Greeks came running up and thrust their spears into Hector's body. Achilles bent down and slit the dead man's heels. He passed a strap through the holes and attached it to his chariot. Then, placing Hector's armour in the chariot, he drove in triumph around the town, dragging the body in the dust. Then he dragged it back to the ships. Here he raised a great pyre and placed the body of his friend Patroclus on it. On the pyre he also burned twelve young Trojan prisoners to appease the spirit of his friend. After this funeral games were held in Patroclus' memory.

Achilles himself had not long to live. Soon afterwards he was struck in his heel by a stray arrow and killed.

The Salamis chariots

For the reconstruction of the chariot from Homer's own time we are on much firmer ground. Several chariot burials have been found at Salamis in Cyprus. From these it is possible to reconstruct a two-man chariot. The chariot box was just under a metre wide and 72 centimetres long. It was divided front to back by a partition to separate the driver from the warrior. The axle was a little over 2 metres long. The wheels were 90 centimetres in diameter. The chariot pole extended 2 metres 20 centimetres in front of the chariot box. It was joined to the yoke by a dowel and probably also bound. Four bronze standards were attached to the yoke bar. The horses themselves had bronze face guards, blinkers and breastplates.

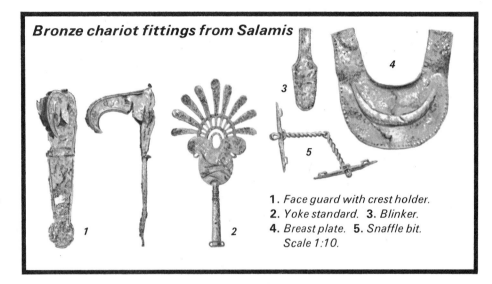

Bronze chariot fittings from Salamis

1. *Face guard with crest holder.*
2. *Yoke standard.* **3.** *Blinker.*
4. *Breast plate.* **5.** *Snaffle bit.*
   Scale 1:10.

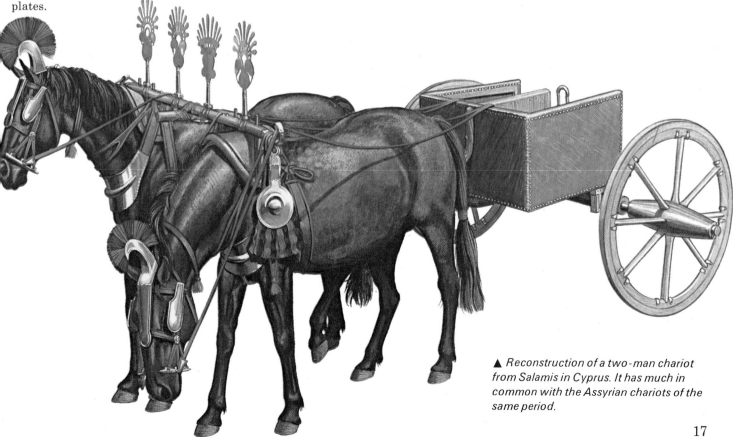

▲ *Reconstruction of a two-man chariot from Salamis in Cyprus. It has much in common with the Assyrian chariots of the same period.*

Warships

The fall of Troy

In spite of their successes the Greeks were unable to take Troy. In the end, according to legend, the crafty Odysseus persuaded the Greeks to build a great wooden horse which they filled with warriors led by Odysseus himself. The rest of the army sailed away, leaving the horse on the shore. The Trojans believed that the horse had been left there by the gods and dragged it into the town. That night Odysseus and his men climbed down from the wooden horse, overpowered the Trojan guards and opened the gates to the rest of the army which had returned after dark.

The discovery at Thera

Until recently our knowledge of Mycenaean ships was exceedingly scant. A few seals and some crude vase paintings were all there was to go on. Then, in 1973, during the excavations on the island of Thera in the Aegean sea, a remarkable discovery was made. Thera had been destroyed by a volcano about 1500 BC. In one of the unearthed buildings a magnificent wall-painting was found. This fresco shows seven beautifully painted warships and a few smaller boats.

The Theran ships

Although this painting tells us an enormous amount about ships of this era, which have a lot in common with Egyptian ships of the same period, they also raise a great many difficulties. For one, the larger ships are being paddled like canoes—a method of propulsion that was obsolete at this period. However, a smaller boat from the same fresco is being rowed. This confusion is compounded by the clearly drawn ram at the rear instead of the front.

It might be suggested that the ship is going in the opposite direction except that the steersman with his large steering oar is at the same end as the ram. The only conclusion that can be drawn is that the boat could be reversed for battle. This could also be the reason that the boat is paddled. A clearly marked Y-shaped protrusion on the prow of two of the ships might be for the steering oar when the boat was reversed. This view is reinforced by the fact that the earliest Greek warships, c. 800–500 BC, all have forecastles.

One of the ships has a mast with long combs at the top on either side for raising the sail. The furled sail rests on the top of the canopy which covered the passengers. The captain sits in a fore/stern castle at the ram end.

▲ Paintings of ships from Thera in the Aegean. The larger ships are being paddled as canoes. The smaller ship is being rowed as a galley. The ships are steered in traditional ancient fashion by large oars at the stern.

▲ A sea peoples' ship shown on an Egyptian carving from Medinet Habu.

The sea peoples

Ships from Greek waters dominated the Mediterranean. In the last days of the Mycenaean civilization great hordes of invaders poured down into the Mediterranean and brought chaos to its shores. These invaders, known as sea peoples, ravaged the eastern Mediterranean coasts and even tried to invade Egypt. The king of Byblos in the Lebanon claimed that he could not ship timber to Egypt because of the sea peoples. Some of these invaders settled along the coasts of the eastern Mediterranean and, mixing with the local people, produced the Philistines and Phoenicians of biblical times.

Troy was taken. The city was sacked and burnt. Some of the inhabitants escaped, the rest were either killed or sold as slaves.

After the fall of Troy the Greeks sailed away to their homeland, which they had not seen for ten years. Odysseus set out with his small fleet of twelve ships but was blown off course by a storm. Driven ashore on the Thracian coast he attacked a town and lost many of his men there. On setting sail again the little fleet was once more driven before the storms and Odysseus and his companions were taken on an unguided tour of the eastern Mediterranean.

Forsaken by the gods, beset by storms and tragedies, one by one Odysseus lost both his men and ships. Finally, after a series of fantastic adventures, in which he claimed he was pursued by monsters, giants and witches, he was shipwrecked on an island having lost every one of his companions. From there, after an absence of twenty years, Odysseus finally managed to reach his homeland, the island of Ithaca. He arrived back to learn of the tragic death of Agamemnon at Mycenae. He also knew that his own life was in danger. Even now his enemies were trying to track him down.

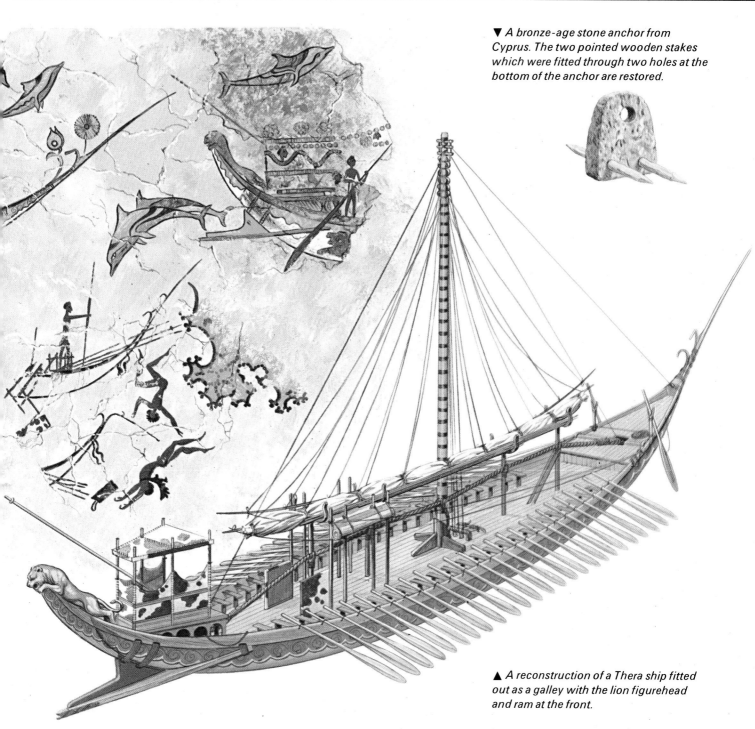

▼ A bronze-age stone anchor from Cyprus. The two pointed wooden stakes which were fitted through two holes at the bottom of the anchor are restored.

▲ A reconstruction of a Thera ship fitted out as a galley with the lion figurehead and ram at the front.

19

Citadels

▲ The citadel of Mycenae as it was in the 13th century BC. In the middle is the Lion Gate with its protecting bastion on the right.

Mycenae and its walls

Several late bronze-age citadels have been excavated in Greece. The most famous of these is Mycenae—the golden citadel of Agamemnon. The palace is built on a rocky hilltop at the edge of the Argive plain. It is surrounded by walls 900 metres long. These walls are typical of a Mycenaean citadel. They are built of massive stones sometimes weighing as much as 12 tonnes. The walls are on average 5 metres thick. The remains of the walls reach a maximum height of 7.5 metres. Originally they were probably 10 to 12 metres high. The total area enclosed by the walls is only about one-sixth of a Roman legionary fortress.

The gates

The wall is pierced by two gates. Both are built at right angles to the wall so that an enemy would come under attack from the walls before the gate could be reached. A bastion was built out from the other side of the gate so that the defenders could bombard the enemy's unshielded side. The main gateway, known as the Lion Gate from the two lions carved in the stone above it, is constructed from four massive stone slabs. The stone which forms the lintel weighs about 20 tonnes. The gateway is about three metres square. It was closed by wooden doors. The holes for the pivots and locking bar are still visible in the stone. The walls are also pierced with two narrow gates through which only one person at a time could pass (sally ports).

The underground cistern

Outside the north-eastern corner of the citadel is an underground cistern which could be approached by a tunnel from inside the walls. Similar underground cisterns exist at Tiryns.

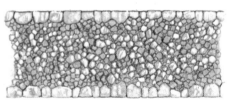

▲ Section through the cyclopean walls showing the stone facing with rubble filling.

▲ The two main types of Mycenaean fortification masonry. The stones were set in clay.
1. Rough cut polygonal stones.
2. Carefully cut rectangular stones.

Tiryns

Tiryns is built on a rocky outcrop rising only 18 metres above the surrounding plain. Its area is about the same as Mycenae. It has galleries with vaulted roofs built into the walls. There is evidence of a mud-brick battlement topping the wall. At this time Hittite and Mesopotamian walls had crenellated battlements. The similarities between Hittite and Mycenaean citadels are numerous and it seems reasonable to assume that Mycenaean walls had hoop-like Hittite crenellations. These crenellations are remarkably Mycenaean in character. The main gate at Tiryns is unique. The entrance is cut straight through the walls. From here it turns left into a narrow passage and passes through a second gate before reaching the courtyard. This gate system is the result of successive extensions producing a citadel within a citadel.

▲ Restored view of the citadel at Tiryns.

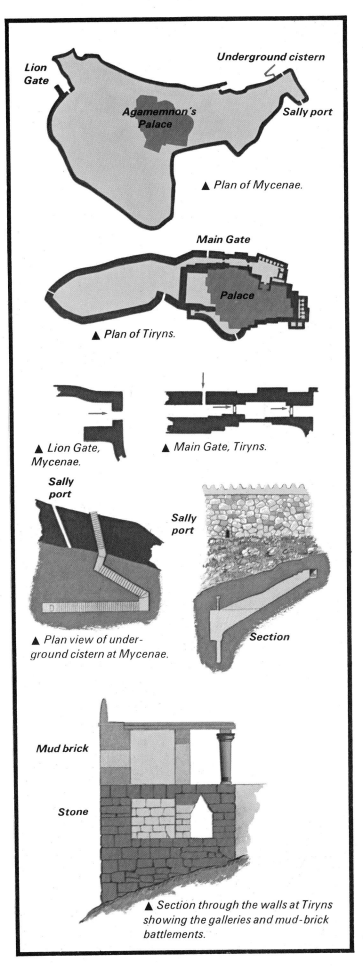

▲ Plan of Mycenae.

▲ Plan of Tiryns.

▲ Lion Gate, Mycenae.

▲ Main Gate, Tiryns.

▲ Plan view of underground cistern at Mycenae.

Section

▲ Section through the walls at Tiryns showing the galleries and mud-brick battlements.

The Twilight of the Mycenaean Age

Odysseus' homecoming

When Odysseus reached Ithaca he heard of Agamemnon's tragic death. Agamemnon had returned to his palace at Mycenae where he was murdered by his wife and her lover. Odysseus also heard that a group of nobles were trying to take over his own kingdom and force his wife to marry one of them. Determined that Agamemnon's fate should not be his, he arrived home disguised as a beggar.

His son, Telemachus, only a baby when Odysseus left for the war, was now a young man. When the two met Odysseus revealed his identity and together they

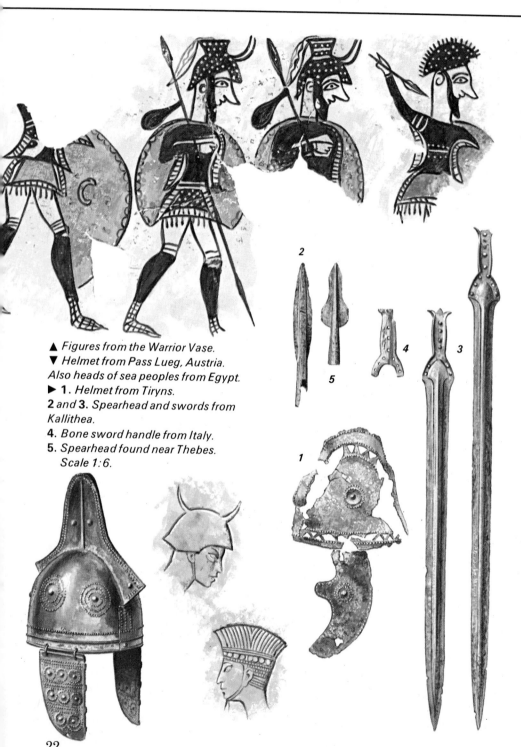

▲ *Figures from the Warrior Vase.*
▼ *Helmet from Pass Lueg, Austria.*
Also heads of sea peoples from Egypt.
▶ **1**. *Helmet from Tiryns.*
2 *and* **3**. *Spearhead and swords from Kallithea.*
4. *Bone sword handle from Italy.*
5. *Spearhead found near Thebes.*
  Scale 1:6.

The fall of Mycenae

Early in the 12th century BC there were great upheavals in the eastern Mediterranean. Egypt and Palestine were invaded, the Hittite empire was overthrown and many of the Mycenaean citadels were destroyed. These events must have happened after the Trojan war. They are probably reflected in the violence that greeted the return of both Agamemnon and Odysseus. The Mycenaean civilization tottered on for a few decades and then collapsed entirely. The reason for these upheavals is uncertain.

The archaeological picture is unclear but it does reveal a change in armament. The Mycenaean tradition seems to end abruptly with the Pylos paintings (p.10). It is succeeded by a foreign weaponry with its origins in central Europe. Mycenaean weaponry survived only in isolated spots such as Athens.

The Warrior Vase

This 12th-century vase is supposed to show Mycenaean warriors from the Trojan-war period. But their long-sleeved jerkins suggest that they come from a colder climate. They carry a crescent-shaped shield which is clearly the *pelta*—the primeval shield of eastern Europe (p. 52).

Their helmets and corselets are drawn in black decorated with white spots. This could be either fabric with metal studs, as was later used in Yugoslavia, or bronze plate with raised bosses. As the helmets have upright crests it is more likely that they were made of bronze with raised bosses. This is a totally un-Mycenaean characteristic but very typical of central Europe. A good parallel is the 12th-century helmet from Pass Lueg in Austria.

The horned helmets and fringed caps shown on the Warrior Vase are reminiscent of those of the sea peoples.

worked out a plan to oust the nobles.

Still disguised as a beggar, Odysseus went to his own palace to beg alms. Here he was abused by the nobles and many of his own servants. Telemachus meanwhile persuaded his unsuspecting mother to marry whichever of her suitors could win a shooting contest with the great hunting bow that hung on the wall. Reluctantly the queen agreed.

The young nobles tried their skill but none of them was able even to string the bow yet alone shoot it. When all had failed the old beggar came forward and asked if he might try. Amidst the mockery of the nobles Odysseus strung the bow and hit the target. Then, throwing off his disguise he turned on the nobles. The nobles fought desperately, but Odysseus' aim was deadly. When all lay still Telemachus took the female servants and hanged them in the courtyard, while Odysseus mutilated his head servant and executed the other male servants in accordance with the brutal practices of his day.

Odysseus' actions meant that he had made the families of his wife's suitors his enemies. He was forced to flee for his life from Ithaca to continue his wanderings.

Weapons

Two swords found at Kallithea are very different from the earlier thrusting weapons. These are Homer's slashing swords. They are of central-European origin and bear no relation to any Mycenaean type. The distribution of this sword suggests a migration from central Europe into both Italy and Greece.

Armour

The embossed egg-shaped greave shown on page 15 was discovered with the two swords from Kallithea. Similar examples have been discovered in central Europe. The graves at Kallithea also produced numerous fragments of bronze decorated with bosses. If these belonged to a cuirass then it was of the Alpine type shown below. The 11th-century embossed helmet from Tiryns fits into this pattern well. The conclusion must be that either there was a northern invasion or that foreign mercenaries were serving in Greece.

Scale armour

Recently a 12th-century bronze scale 5 centimetres by 2 centimetres was excavated at Mycenae. This scale is of Assyrian type. Parallels have been found in Cyprus and various sites in the Middle East, including Troy. It could be argued that this is the remains of a trophy brought back from the Trojan war. However, the use of this type of armour was widespread.

▲ 1. *Pieces of embossed bronze from Kallithea.*
2. *12th-century scale from Mycenae. Scale 1:3.*
▶ *Late bronze-age cuirass from Switzerland.*

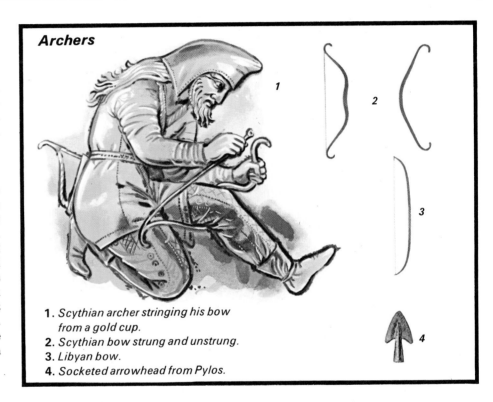

Archers

1. *Scythian archer stringing his bow from a gold cup.*
2. *Scythian bow strung and unstrung.*
3. *Libyan bow.*
4. *Socketed arrowhead from Pylos.*

Bowmen

The bowmen shown in Mycenaean art carry the Libyan bow. This bow, like the cupid's bow of the Scythians which became so popular in the classical period, is made of wood reinforced with horn and sinew. This type of bow was very difficult to string and required the use of both arms and legs. For when unstrung the two "horns" curved forward. None of the suitors was able to string Odysseus' bow. In the *Iliad* the bow is scarcely respectable and no hero would stoop to using it in battle.

No remains of bows have been found. The dart and tanged type of arrow head remained in use. Socketed arrowheads have also been found.

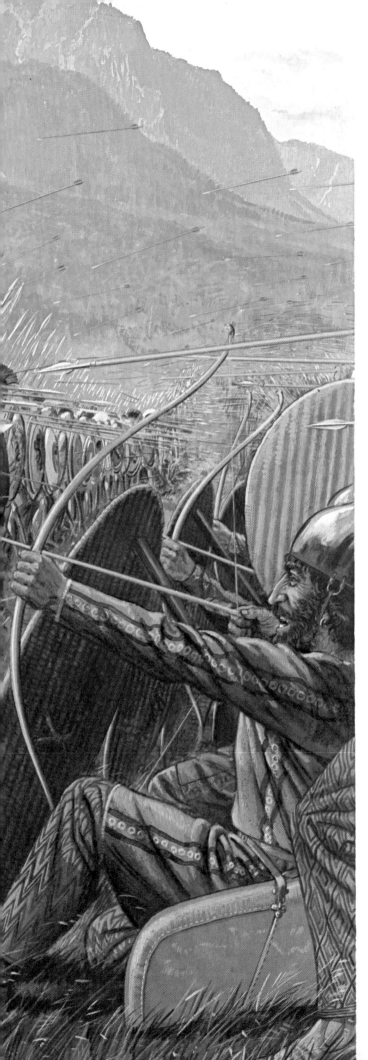

The Age of the City States

Greece in 700–350 BC was very different from the Mycenaean Greece of 1600–1300 BC. During the 7th to 4th centuries BC the whole of Greece was divided into tiny warring states, each centred around a town. The period was dominated first by the Persian invasions, and later by the bitter war between Sparta and Athens. It is fortunate that there were two great historians living during this period who provide us with a wealth of information. Herodotus lived at the time of the Persian invasion of Greece, and Thucydides was involved in the war between Athens and Sparta. There was also Xenophon who lived towards the end of the period. Although he was not as great a writer as Herodotus and Thucydides, he was a soldier who provides an incomparable source of military information.

These literary sources are supported by a mass of archaeological evidence. After a battle it was customary for the victor to dedicate some armour in one of the sanctuaries at Olympia. These shrines became so filled with armour that many older pieces had to be removed. Some were just dumped in streams and disused wells, other pieces were used to reinforce the banks of the stadium. Recently much of this armour has been excavated.

At the end of the 6th century BC the mighty Persian army came thundering down on what is now Turkey. The many Greek colonies there appealed to Greece for help, and expeditionary forces were sent to their aid. In retaliation Persia launched an attack against Greece itself, and so the great Persian wars began.

◀ *The last charge of the Spartans at Thermopylae. Leonidas and the remnants of his tiny army advance into the open ground determined to fight to the death.*

The Phalanx

The battle of Marathon

In 490 BC the Persian fleet launched an attack against Greece. Faced with foreign invasion, Athens and Sparta buried their differences and united against the common enemy.

The Persian army disembarked about 50 kilometres north of Athens and laid siege to Eretria. The Athenians sent to Sparta for help and set out to relieve Eretria. The Persians then moved part of their army down the coast to threaten Athens itself. Near the town of Marathon the two armies came face to face. The Athenians dared not risk a battle

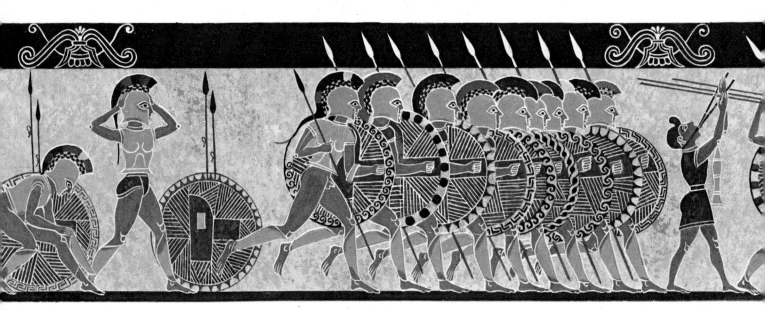

▲ This 7th-century Corinthian vase shows hoplites being piped into battle. It gives a clear representation of the early phalanx. The hoplites are wearing the bell cuirass and short greaves and carrying spears which could be thrown in Homeric fashion.

The new formation

During the 8th century there was a revolution in the Greek method of warfare. The free-for-all fighting of the heroic age was abandoned, and a far more disciplined system, the phalanx, was introduced. The phalanx was a long block of soldiers several ranks deep. There were usually eight ranks, but there could be as few as four, or many more than eight. The phalanx was organized in files (lines from front to back) so that when a man fell his place was taken by the man behind. (8 ranks of 100=100 files of 8.) The phalanx would be drawn up in open order with 1.5 to 2 metres per man, or doubled up to form close order.

This way of fighting was made possible by a new shield (see p.30). This round shield, held across the chest, covered a warrior from chin to knees. When the phalanx was in close order, the shield was wide enough to protect the unguarded side of the man on the left.

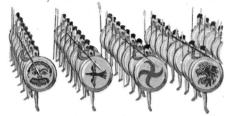

▲ The phalanx in open order. The front rank is made up of file leaders.

▲ The phalanx in close order. It is made up of half files.

Arms

The new type of warrior was called a hoplite (armoured man). He wore a bronze helmet, cuirass and greaves. By the time of the Persian invasion the bronze cuirass had been replaced by a linen one.

In the 8th-7th centuries he was still armed with two "Homeric" throwing spears, but soon after he adopted the long thrusting spear and a short sword.

Athenian hoplites

All Athenian men between the ages of 17 and 59 were liable for military service. During the 5th century there were about 30,000 Athenian hoplites, nearly half of whom were campaign soldiers. The remainder, those under 19 and the veterans, performed garrison duties. Hoplites were from wealthy families, as only they could afford the equipment. A soldier whose father was killed in battle was armed at public expense.

without Spartan help.

After the news of the fall of Eretria came, the Athenians realized that the rest of the Persian army would soon arrive. They could not wait for the Spartans, so the *stratgegos* ordered the attack. Singing their war song, keeping pace to the flutes, the hoplites charged. In the centre the Persians smashed the Greek line, but on both wings the Athenians were victorious. The Persians turned and fled. The Athenian wings now wheeled round and caught the Persian centre in a pincers movement. 6,400 Persians died, whereas the Athenians lost only 192 men.

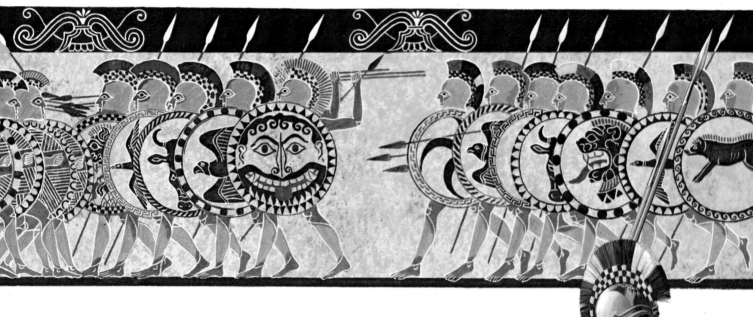

Officers

In the democratic states the general (*strategos*) was probably elected. In Athens ten generals were elected. Usually only three went with the army. One of the three was made commander-in-chief, or each commanded in turn.

The army was divided into ten tribes, which in turn were divided into companies. Each company (*lochos*) was probably split up into files, each with its own leader as in Sparta (see p.29). Officers served in the front rank at the right-hand side of the company they commanded. As all officers were front-rank men, the losses in battle must have been enormous, and as a result promotion very quick.

Few generals survived failure. In Athens, unsuccessful generals were often put on trial and banished, fined, imprisoned or even condemned to death. In Carthage they were regularly crucified and their families disgraced for generations.

Heralds

Each army had heralds whose job was to convey the general's orders down the chain of command, or to carry messages between warring states. As the time and place for battle was often agreed in advance, a herald would be sent to make these arrangements. When states were on bad terms they might only communicate through their heralds.

Augurs

The augurs or priests were also considered of great importance. Although some generals fixed the omens to suit their own ends, no pious general would dream of fighting if the omens were unfavourable. At Plataea the Spartan general refused to fight even though the Persians were attacking his men. Xenophon admitted that he would not move his men because of unfavourable omens, even though they were faced with starvation.

▲ A hoplite of about 600 BC. He is wearing a Corinthian helmet, bell cuirass and short greaves.

27

Sparta: A Military State

For ten years the Greeks were free from the Persian threat. However, everyone knew that the Persians would attempt another invasion. Therefore alliances were formed and Athens built up her fleet.

In the spring of 480 BC, the Persian king Xerxes invaded Europe with a vast army. Athens and Sparta again united, the Athenians surrendering the command of their entire forces to the Spartans.

It was decided to try to block the massive Persian army at the narrow pass of Thermopylae, about 150 kilometres north of Athens. The hills there descend

▲ A Spartan hoplite about 500 B.C. He wears a Corinthian helmet, linen corselet and full-length greaves.

A military state

Sparta was the most feared state in Greece. It was accepted as a fact that one Spartan was worth several men of any other state. None of the other states, unless forced, would dare oppose Sparta on the battlefield.

Everything in Sparta was regulated by the state. All Spartan men were soldiers; other professions were forbidden to them. Food was provided by dividing the land into farms which were worked by slaves. Each Spartan was allocated to one of these farms and took his livelihood from it, without having to work it himself. The rigorous training of a Spartan began before birth, expectant mothers having to perform strenuous exercises to ensure their babies were strong. Weak babies were killed.

Childhood

At the age of seven boys were taken from their mothers. They were grouped into classes, where they lived, ate and slept together, all ruled by the same discipline.

The boys were taught by mature and experienced citizens of Sparta. The academic education was minimal, as the emphasis was on discipline and exercise. For the most part children went barefoot and naked, again to make them stronger and tougher. Their food was always simple and scant, so that they would be encouraged to steal. Although children were punished when they were caught stealing, the punishment was for being caught, not for stealing. This was to train the boys, so that as soldiers they might be able to endure famine and forage for themselves.

At the age of twelve the discipline became much harsher. The boys were permanently burdened with hard work and exercises.

Bravery and cowardice

Fighting was encouraged among both adults and children, provided the fight was not in anger. A fight had to break up if ordered so by another citizen. A boy was thrashed by his father because he complained that another boy had hit him.

The Spartans considered bravery the greatest virtue and cowardice the worst vice. Children were taught this from an early age. There is a fine story of a Spartan mother telling her son that he must return from battle either carrying his shield or lying on it. For when the dead were removed from the battlefield they were carried on their shields. On the other hand, the first thing a hoplite would discard when running away in battle would be his heavy shield.

A boy reached manhood in his twentieth year, when he became a soldier. As the Spartan army was organized by age groups the young men continued to live together. Even when they were married Spartan men lived and ate in the barracks without their wives.

Slaves and allies

During the 9th–8th centuries Sparta gradually conquered her neighbouring states. Some of these states were allowed a form of self-government, but they were always compelled to fight as Sparta's allies. Most conquered people were made slaves (helots). One of the reasons that made it necessary to run Sparta as a military state was the large number of slaves.

The kings

Supreme power was in the hands of two hereditary kings who led the army in battle. Originally both kings went on campaigns, but shortly before the Persian wars it was restricted to only one. Each king had a special bodyguard of 100 soldiers (hippeis).

steeply into the pass leaving only a narrow passage-way along the marshy coast. Offshore the long island of Euboea forms a narrow channel stretching about 150 kilometres along the coast.

The Greek plan was to oppose the Persian army in the pass in the belief that Xerxes would be forced to use his fleet to break through. When this happened the Greek fleet would be able to engage the Persians in the narrows. Accordingly most of the Greek fleet, about 300 triremes, advanced to Artemisium at the head of the Euboean channel.

The Spartan king, Leonidas, marched northwards with 4,000 southern Greeks and 300 Spartans. On the way he was joined by about 4,000 other hoplites. These troops joined believing that they were only the advance guard of the combined Greek army. When they reached the pass the army repaired an old wall across it and they planned their defence around this wall.

When Xerxes heard that a Greek army occupied the pass, as expected, he ordered his fleet to sail further down the coast and take the Greeks from the rear. For four days Xerxes waited, but his fleet failed to get past the Greek navy.

The organization of the Spartan Army

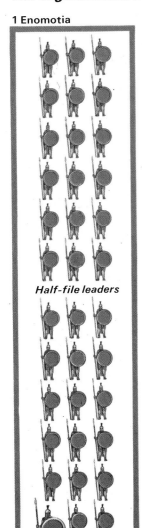

1 Enomotia

Half-file leaders

File leaders

Enomotarch

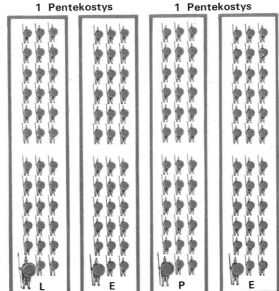

Lochos

1 Pentekostys   **1 Pentekostys**

L   E   P   E

▲ *A* lochos *composed of two* pente-kostyes, *each made up of two* enomotiai. *It is commanded by a* lochagos.
L = Lochagos
E = Enomotarch
P = Pentekonter

◄ *An* enomotia *of 36 men commanded by an* enomotarch. *It is divided into three files or six half-files.*

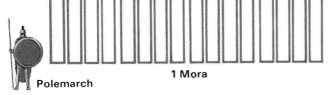

Polemarch

1 Mora

▲ *A mora composed of four* lochoi *and commanded by a* polemarch.

Spartan Army = 6 Morae

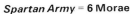

King

The scarlet cloak
All men between the ages of 20 and 60 were soldiers. Spartan hoplites were armed in the same way as other Greeks, but in addition they wore a scarlet cloak. This cloak became the symbol of Spartan militarism.

The army
Thucydides and Xenophon give contra-dictory accounts of the organization of the Spartan army. On Spartan matters Xenophon must be accepted as the greater authority as he had first-hand experience. According to Xenophon, Spartan hoplites were organized into files. Each file (enomotia) was commanded by an enomotarch. Files were linked to form "fifties" (pentekostyes), each with its own commander. Two fifties were joined to form a lochos, the smallest tactical unit of the army. The lochos was commanded by a lochagos.

The whole Spartan army was composed of six divisions. Each division (mora) was commanded by a polemarch and contained four lochoi.

The army was called up by age groups starting with the youngest. The veterans were only called up in an emergency, when they only guarded the baggage train.

The declining population
The Spartan population was constantly declining. Between the 7th and the beginning of the 5th centuries the army strength dropped from 9,000 to 8,000 and a hundred years later it was only 3,600. It is impossible to state the size of a unit. Here, an enomotia has been put at 36 men. The number of lochoi to a mora probably varied as well.

Drill and Battle Tactics

The struggle for the pass

On the fifth day Xerxes decided to send forward part of his infantry with orders to bring the Greeks back alive. All day long the battle raged in the pass until at dusk the defeated Persians dragged themselves back. The following morning Xerxes sent his personal bodyguard, the Immortals, to fight the Greeks, but they too were cut to pieces.

That night a traitor led some of the Persians around the pass by a secret path through the densely wooded hills. Leonidas had foreseen this possibility and had left a thousand men to guard the path. These soldiers

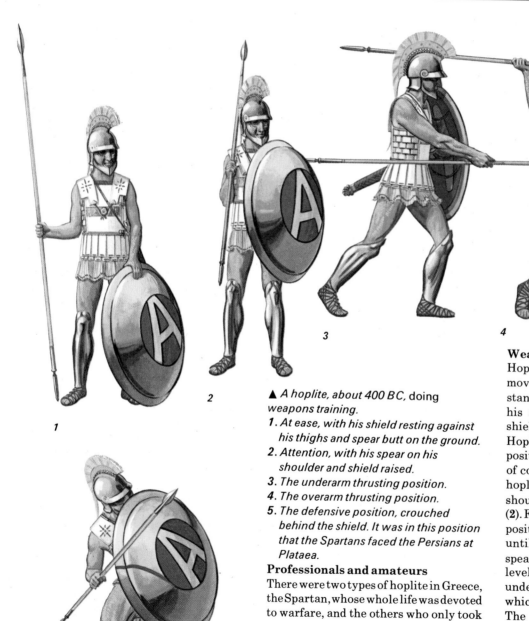

▲ *A hoplite, about 400 B C, doing weapons training.*
1. *At ease, with his shield resting against his thighs and spear butt on the ground.*
2. *Attention, with his spear on his shoulder and shield raised.*
3. *The underarm thrusting position.*
4. *The overarm thrusting position.*
5. *The defensive position, crouched behind the shield. It was in this position that the Spartans faced the Persians at Plataea.*

Professionals and amateurs

There were two types of hoplite in Greece, the Spartan, whose whole life was devoted to warfare, and the others who only took up arms in an emergency. The drill shown on this page is confined to Spartan practices only. The other states used the simpler manoeuvres; the more complicated ones were probably never attempted outside Sparta.

Weapon training

Hoplites were instructed in a few basic movements with spear and shield. When standing at ease the hoplite stood with his spear butt on the ground and his shield resting against his thighs (1). Hoplites would sometimes retain this position in the face of the enemy as a sign of contempt. When called to attention a hoplite raised his spear to his right shoulder and his shield to cover his torso (2). From there he adopted the "on-guard" position by bringing his spear forwards until his right arm was straight and the spear parallel to the ground at waist level (3). This was the position for the underarm thrust and the position in which the hoplite advanced into battle. The hoplite took up the more common overarm thrusting position by reversing his grip and raising the spear above his head (4). This was the normal fighting attitude in close order. There was also the defensive position, crouched behind the shield (5).

were wakened by the sound of the Persians approaching. Misunderstanding the aim of the Persian force they withdrew to a stronger position leaving the path open.

When Leonidas heard this news he realized he had no hope of victory. He sent away most of his allies. Only 1,100 Thespians and Thebans remained with Leonidas and his Spartans.

Xerxes waited until mid-morning before entering the pass. Leonidas, realizing that he could not hold his position, advanced in phalanx to where the pass was wider.

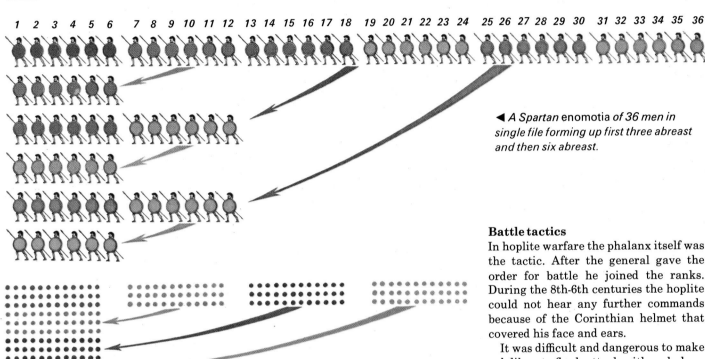

◀ A Spartan enomotia of 36 men in single file forming up first three abreast and then six abreast.

▲ A lochos (four enomotiai) drawn up three men abreast moving forwards to form a phalanx twelve wide.

Drill

Young Spartan soldiers were first taught to march in single file. When they had mastered this they were taught to form up in columns of various depths. For example, a unit of 36 men (enomotia) was selected. The first man commanded the whole unit, the 13th man commanded numbers 14 to 24, and the 25th man commanded numbers 26 to 36. On the order to form up three abreast, the 13th and 25th men brought forward their twelves at two-metre intervals on the left, or shield side, of numbers 1 to 12 (see above). Similarly to form a front of six, the 7th, 19th and 31st men brought up the five men behind them. This formed a block of men six wide and six deep. To reform a single file this was reversed.

Forming the phalanx

When a lochos (four enomotiai) marching three men abreast was given the order to form a phalanx the first enomotia halted. The three enomotiai behind moved up on the left to form a block 12 men wide and 12 men deep, with 2 metres between files. This was open order. To form close order the rear half of each file moved forward into the space on the left of the front half of the file. Other lochoi moved up in a similar way on the left of the first lochos. If the enemy appeared in the rear each file counter-marched. The officer turned about and the rest of his unit re-formed behind him. When the instructions were issued by the commander the movements were executed at the sound of a trumpet.

Battle tactics

In hoplite warfare the phalanx itself was the tactic. After the general gave the order for battle he joined the ranks. During the 8th-6th centuries the hoplite could not hear any further commands because of the Corinthian helmet that covered his face and ears.

It was difficult and dangerous to make a deliberate flank attack with a phalanx for it was impossible to "wheel". It involved turning part of the phalanx into a marching column, and then taking up a new position at right angles to the rest of the line. If the enemy attacked while the phalanx was re-forming it could have disastrous results.

At the battle of Marathon the Athenians caught the Persians in a double pincers movement. Although a similar tactic was used in the sea battle of Salamis, it appears to have been used by chance and not design at Marathon.

The attack

On the order to attack the trumpet sounded and the hoplites advanced in the "on-guard" position, singing their war song (paean). The advance kept step to the sound of flutes. As the hoplites approached the enemy the trumpet sounded the charge, a cheer was raised and the soldiers broke into a run.

Shields

Death at Thermopylae

The Persians rushed upon the Greek line in a great mass. Again and again the Greeks beat them off. The slaughter was so great that the Persians had to climb over piles of their dead to reach the Greeks. The tiny Greek army fought on until their spears were shattered and they could fight only with their swords. Leonidas was killed in the struggle, but his companions fought on over his body.

At midday news came that the Persians were advancing from the other end of the pass. When the surviving Greeks heard this they withdrew to a small

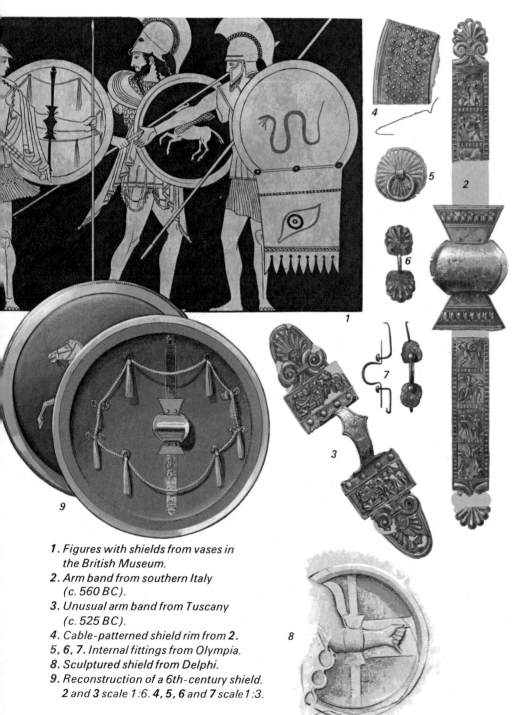

1. Figures with shields from vases in the British Museum.
2. Arm band from southern Italy (c. 560 BC).
3. Unusual arm band from Tuscany (c. 525 BC).
4. Cable-patterned shield rim from 2.
5, 6, 7. Internal fittings from Olympia.
8. Sculptured shield from Delphi.
9. Reconstruction of a 6th-century shield.
   2 and 3 scale 1:6. 4, 5, 6 and 7 scale 1:3.

The new shield

The Mycenaean figure-eight type of shield remained in use until the 8th century in the areas of Greece that survived the upheavals of the 12th century BC (see p.22). The Dorians, who settled in southern Greece c. 1050 BC, probably brought with them a round shield with a central handgrip. During the 8th century this round shield was modified: an arm-band was fixed in the centre and the handgrip moved nearer the rim. It was this shield that made the rigid phalanx formation possible. Half the shield protruded beyond the left-hand side of the warrior. If the man on the left moved in close he was protected by the shield overlap which guarded his uncovered side. Later the shield sometimes had a leather curtain hanging down to protect the warrior's legs from darts and arrows.

The shields from Olympia

After a battle it was customary for the victorious general to dedicate an inscribed shield at one of the sanctuaries. Many such shields have been found at Olympia. Some have a complete bronze facing, others have only a bronze rim. All the non-metallic parts of these shields have disappeared, although many of the interior fittings have been discovered. The fittings were fixed to the core of the shield with rivets, which were bent over on the front. The core of the shield was wooden, faced with bronze or ox hide.

Several shields from Olympia have fittings stuck directly on to the back of the bronze facing. These shields were made specially for dedications as they would have been useless in battle. It has been suggested that they were used to deflect blows, but this would defeat the whole purpose of the phalanx. Each hoplite was supposed to protect his neighbour's unguarded side, not redirect missiles on to it.

hillock and formed a square. Here they defended themselves with their swords and fists, until Xerxes ordered his infantry to withdraw and his archers to attack. The Greeks crouched behind their shields to protect themselves from the arrows. By early afternoon all was still. The pass was strewn with bodies. Leonidas' men were all dead, but their courage was to live for ever.

When the tragic news of this defeat reached the Greek fleet, they decided to withdraw. Although they had engaged the Persian fleet twice, they had failed to gain a victory. They withdrew to the channel behind the island of Salamis, just off the Athenian coast. The city of Athens was evacuated except for a group of men left to defend the Acropolis. These men were all killed when the Acropolis was captured and burnt by the Persians. All the Athenian men moved to Salamis and the women and children were ferried to the southern mainland at Troezen.

The road along the isthmus that led to southern Greece was broken up and a wall built across the narrowest point near Corinth, as the last Mycenaeans had done in similar circumstances 700 years before.

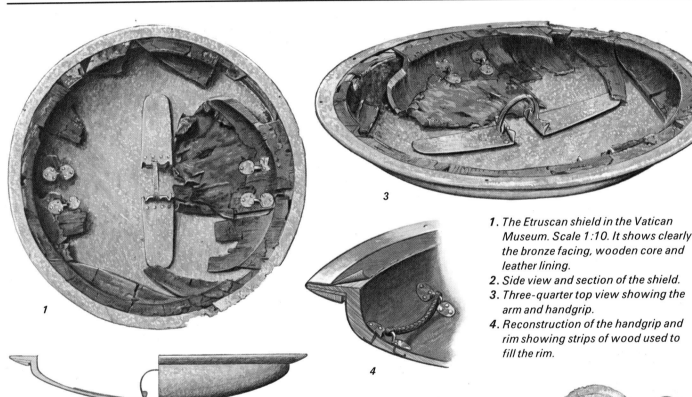

1. The Etruscan shield in the Vatican Museum. Scale 1:10. It shows clearly the bronze facing, wooden core and leather lining.
2. Side view and section of the shield.
3. Three-quarter top view showing the arm and handgrip.
4. Reconstruction of the handgrip and rim showing strips of wood used to fill the rim.

The Vatican shield
The only good example of a true battle shield is in the Vatican museum, probably from an Etruscan grave. It is the most complete shield yet discovered. It dates from the end of the 5th century and is made of wood with a complete bronze facing. The inside was lined with thin leather.

The wooden core of the shield was quite thin in the centre. A reinforcing plate was often fixed on the inside. These plates can be seen clearly on the Chigi vase (p. 26) and the Delphi relief (left).

Shield motifs
The most noticeable feature of the hoplon shield is its motif. These could be legs, anchors, animals or mythical creatures. Several examples of bronze motifs have been found at Olympia. They were probably made specially for the dedications, as they would have been defaced at the first clash in battle. The motifs on battle shields were painted.

Towards the end of the 5th century the motif was replaced by a letter identifying the hoplite's city.

▲ A bronze shield motif from Olympia c. 525 BC. The gorgon was the most popular shield motif.

Helmets and Weapons

700 BC

650 BC

600 BC

550 BC

500 BC

Types of Greek helmet
There are several forms of Greek helmet, but they all seem to have evolved from two main types—the Kegel (**1**) and the primitive Corinthian (**2**).

Kegel, Illyrian and Insular
The Kegel was made in several pieces. It was not very successful and died out at the beginning of the 7th century. From the Kegel evolved the Insular helmet (**3**), which was also short lived, and the early Illyrian (**4**). The Illyrian continued to be used in varying forms (**5**, **6** and **7**) until the 5th century.

Corinthian
The Corinthian was by far the most successful Greek helmet. It covered the face leaving only the eyes clear. It had a long life, beginning in the 8th century (**2**) and evolving into a very elegant helmet during the 7th and 6th centuries (**8**, **9**, **10**, **11** and **12**). There was a slight variant, known as the Myros type (**9**) during the late 7th and early 6th centuries. There was also a cross-breed, which had an Illyrian-style crest ridge (**10**).

Etrusco–Corinthian
The Corinthian helmet died out in Greece early in the 5th century. When the soldier was not fighting he could push the Corinthian helmet on to the top of his head. The Italians began wearing the helmet pushed up like this when they went into battle, and developed what is known as the Etrusco–Corinthian helmet (**13**, **14** and **15**). Soon the eye holes became so small and close together (**15**) that it would be impossible to see through them. The helmet finally disappeared in the 1st century AD.

Chalcidian and Attic
The Corinthian helmet had one great fault—it made hearing impossible. Experiments were made with ear holes (**16**), but a better helmet, the Chalcidian, then evolved that left both the mouth and ears clear. This helmet comes in two types: one with fixed cheek pieces (**17**) and one with hinged ones (**18**).

The Attic helmet (**19**) was a variant of the Chalcidian and had no nose guard. It was very popular in Italy, where many examples have survived; these usually had feather holders, and often wings.

Thracian
The Thracian helmet (**20**) became very popular during the 5th century and continued in use until the 2nd century. It had a peak at the front and long pointed cheek pieces, usually cut away at the mouth and eyes. The cheek pieces were often highly decorated with, for example, a beard and moustache.

1. The two types of crest.
2. A Greek raised crest-holder.
3. An Italian raised crest-holder.
Both 2 and 3 were secured by split pins.

Crests
Crests made of horse hair were an essential feature of Greek helmets. Most crests fitted directly on to the helmet, tied to a pin at the back and front. Crests raised on a prop were often used during the Archaic period, 700 to 500 BC. They remained popular in Italy until the 1st century AD.

Lining
Helmets and all other armour were lined with leather, linen or felt. The lining was often turned over the edge and stitched like the Dendra armour, but from the 6th century onwards it was more often glued in.

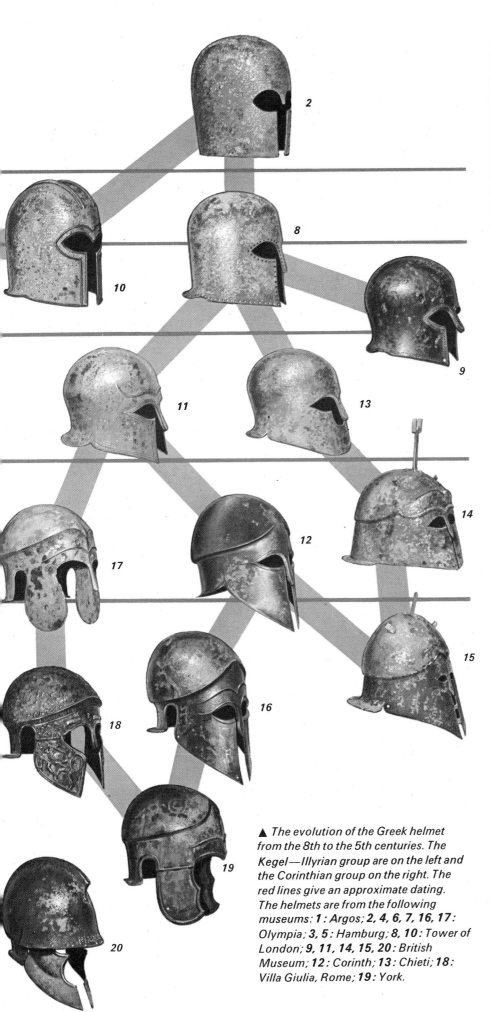

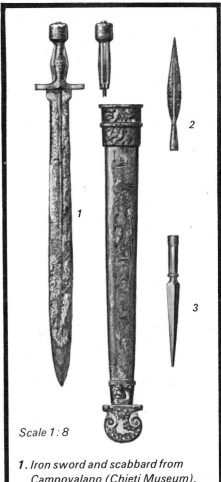

Scale 1 : 8

1. *Iron sword and scabbard from Campovalano (Chieti Museum).*
2. *Iron spearhead from Campovalano (Chieti Museum).*
3. *Bronze spear butt (British Museum*

▲ *The evolution of the Greek helmet from the 8th to the 5th centuries. The Kegel—Illyrian group are on the left and the Corinthian group on the right. The red lines give an approximate dating. The helmets are from the following museums: 1 : Argos; 2, 4, 6, 7, 16, 17 : Olympia; 3, 5 : Hamburg; 8, 10 : Tower of London; 9, 11, 14, 15, 20 : British Museum; 12 : Corinth; 13 : Chieti; 18 : Villa Giulia, Rome; 19 : York.*

Spears

The hoplite's main weapon was the spear. From Greek vases it seems that the spears were about 2 to 3 metres long. By the end of the 8th century, the Greeks no longer buried their warriors with their weapons, but the practice continued in Italy. Spears varying from between 1.5 metres and 2.5 metres have been found in 6th-century graves at Campovalano near Chieti. The spears on Greek vases have leaf-shaped blades, many spears like this have been found in both Greece and Italy. Spears also had a metal spike, often made of bronze, at the butt end.

Swords

Hoplites also carried a short sword. This had a leaf-shaped blade about 60 centimetres long. Several excellent examples have been found at Campovalano. The curved sword *(kopis)*, which became increasingly popular during the 5th and 4th centuries, is shown on page 61.

35

Bronze Cuirasses

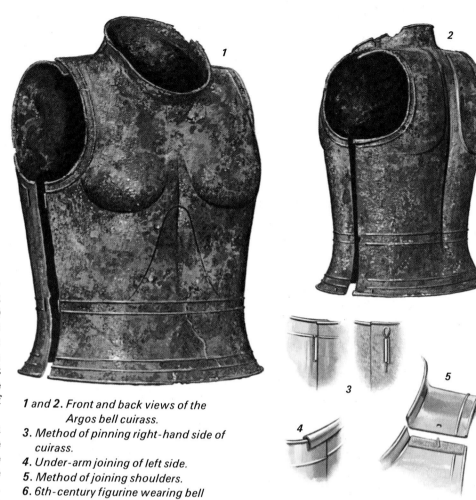

1 *and* **2**. *Front and back views of the Argos bell cuirass.*

3. *Method of pinning right-hand side of cuirass.*

4. *Under-arm joining of left side.*

5. *Method of joining shoulders.*

6. *6th-century figurine wearing bell cuirass.*

7. *Late bell cuirass from Olympia, c. 525 BC.*

The bell cuirass

In 1953 an 8th-century grave was excavated at Argos in southern Greece. In it were the earliest Greek helmet (p.35,**1**) and cuirass yet found. This cuirass ends a gap of 700 years since the Dendra armour (p.12). This early cuirass is known as the "bell" from its shape. It became the standard equipment of the hoplite, and is shown on hundreds of Greek vases and sculptures.

The Argos cuirass has a front and back plate. On the right edge of the front plate are two tubular projections. These were fitted into corresponding slots in the back plate before putting the cuirass on. They were held in place by two pins on the inside (**3**). On the left side the two halves were strapped together by two loops at the bottom. Under the left arm and at the bottom, the edge of the back plate is folded over to hold the front plate in position (**4**). There were two spikes at the shoulders of the front plate which passed through corresponding holes in the back (**5**).

▲ *An abdominal plate from Crete.*

Abdominal plates

A semi-circular bronze plate could be suspended from a belt to cover the abdomen. Although there are some Greek examples of these, most of them come from Crete.

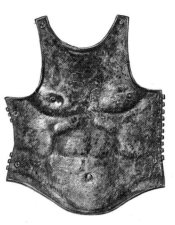

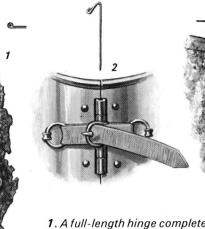

1. A full-length hinge complete with pin (Karlsruhe Museum).
2. Method of pulling hinges together.
3. A hinge from the inside.
4. A fragment of a cuirass with ring attachment and traces of a buckle (British Museum).
5. A buckle of similar type.

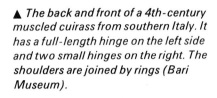

▲ *The back and front of a 4th-century muscled cuirass from southern Italy. It has a full-length hinge on the left side and two small hinges on the right. The shoulders are joined by rings (Bari Museum).*

▶ *A reconstruction of a muscled cuirass with silver inset nipples (British Museum).*

The muscled cuirass

In the middle of the 6th century, the bell cuirass was abandoned in favour of the linen cuirass (see p.38). However a new type of bronze cuirass evolved. Although it was never as popular as the bell cuirass it lasted until the end of the Roman era, a thousand years later. This was the elegant muscled cuirass which became part of the uniform of senior officers. It was either short, finishing at the waist, or long to cover the abdomen. The short type was often used by cavalry.

The muscled cuirass was usually joined at the sides and sometimes at the shoulders by hinges. The two halves of the hinge were pushed together and the pin inserted. On either side of the hinge was a ring, which was used to pull the front and back together. A fragment in the British Museum (4) shows the clear impression of a buckle next to the ring, proving that a strap and buckle were used to pull the two sides together.

Some 4th-century cuirasses have the left-hand hinge extending from the armpit to the hip. The left side was probably fastened before putting the cuirass on, as it would be impossible to insert the pin under the arm.

Although muscled cuirasses are shown on Greek vases, the archaeological examples come mainly from Italy.

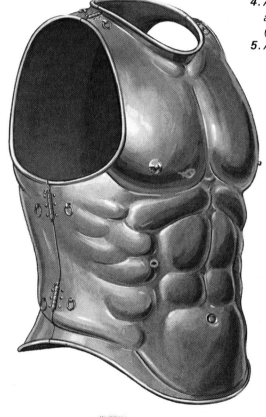

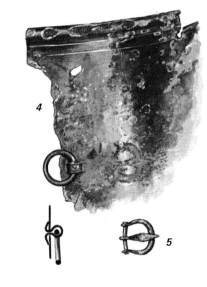

▲ *A short muscled cuirass with rings and no hinges (British Museum).*

◀ *A vase painting showing a hoplite in a muscled cuirass, c. 460 BC.*

Linen Cuirasses, Arm, Leg and Foot Guards

The linen cuirass

Linen cuirasses had probably been used since late Mycenaean times; but it was not until late in the 6th century that they became the standard armour of the hoplite. A linen cuirass was made of many layers of linen glued together to form a stiff shirt, about half a centimetre thick. The lower part had slits to make it easier to bend down, a second layer cut into similar strips (*pteryges*) was placed on the inside to cover the gaps in the outer layer. The shirt was wrapped around the torso and tied together on the left side. A U-shaped piece, fixed to the back, was pulled forward to cover the shoulders. These cuirasses were often made in several pieces and the *pteryges* were sometimes detachable.

Although linen was considered adequate protection, these cuirasses were often reinforced with scales or plates. Assyrian-style lamellar plates are shown on later Etruscan cuirasses.

The great advantage of the linen cuirass was its flexibility. It remained in use until the introduction of mail in about 250 BC.

▲ The linen cuirass in Greek and Etruscan art.
1. Greek, c. 510 BC.
2. Etruscan, c. 425 BC.
3. Greek, c. 450 BC.
4. Lamellar plates shown on an Etruscan bronze statue, c. 350 BC.
5. From an Etruscan painting, c. 325 BC.

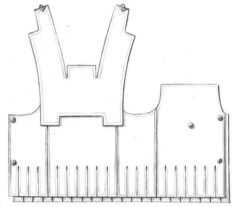

◄ The cut of a linen "stiff-shirt" cuirass.

▲ *A vase painting of the 6th century showing hoplites dressing.*

◄ *A late 6th-century warrior putting on his linen cuirass.*

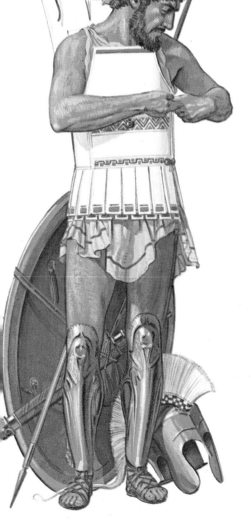

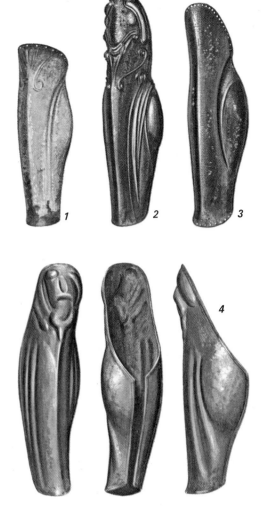

▲ *The development of the greave.*
1. Late 7th century.
2 and 3. 6th century.
4. c. 500 BC.

▼ *1. Upper arm guard.*
2. Lower arm guard.
3. Ankle guard.
4. Thigh guard.
5. Foot guard.

Greaves

The full-length lower leg guard, or greave, came into general use in the 7th century. At first it covered only the lower leg, but was later extended to cover the knee. The 7th- and 6th-century greaves were often highly decorated. The later greaves, like the muscled cuirass, followed the anatomy of the leg. There are many examples of muscled greaves from both Italy and Greece. The greave was pulled open and clipped round the leg. In Italy many greaves have been found with rings for straps.

Ankle, thigh and foot guards

Many examples of guards to cover the ankles and heels, have been found, but there are few examples of foot guards. Foot guards were either made in one piece or hinged at the toes. Although thigh guards are shown in sculptures, only one example has been found in Greece, at Olympia.

Upper and lower arm guards

Guards for both upper and lower arm have been discovered at Olympia. There are many more upper arm guards than lower ones. Some are very elaborately decorated. Arm guards were probably very seldom used, as they are rarely shown in paintings. All these additional arm and leg guards disappeared at the end of the 6th century.

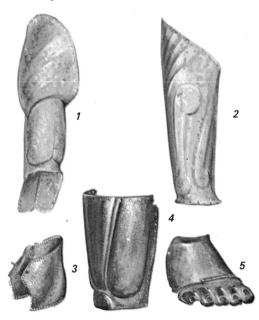

Early Warships

The Persian fleet strikes

After his victory over Leonidas and his Greek army Xerxes left Thermopylae and advanced on Athens. The Athenians watched helplessly from Salamis as the column of smoke betrayed the destruction of their beloved city.

The Persian fleet then rounded the southernmost point of Attica and moved up towards Salamis. Panic swept through the Greek fleet. The southern Greeks were frightened that if they were defeated at Salamis they would be cut off from their homeland. They wanted to withdraw and make a stand at Corinth.

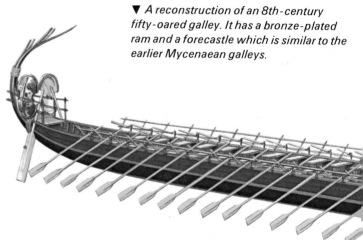

▼ A reconstruction of an 8th-century fifty-oared galley. It has a bronze-plated ram and a forecastle which is similar to the earlier Mycenaean galleys.

▲ Ships from two early vase paintings showing galleys. Both these probably represent the same type of galley with rowers at one level.

▲ An 8th-century fire dog made in the shape of an early galley. This came from the same grave at Argos as the cuirass on page 36.

1. Stone anchor from Piraeus.
2. Lead anchor stock.
3. Admiralty-type anchor shown on a 6th-century shield.

The ships of Homer's time

The ships described by Homer are almost certainly those of his own day. These ships are of two types: light, fast ships of twenty oars and heavier warships with fifty oars. They are unquestionably galleys and not canoes as thole pins with leather loops for holding the oars are often mentioned. These ships have benches for the oarsmen. Odysseus drags one of his drunken comrades aboard and leaves him "beneath the benches".

These boats are made from pine wood and their oars of polished fir. When at sea they could be anchored with a large stone tied to a rope. The conventional admiralty-type anchor came in about 600 BC. At night, whenever possible, ships would be dragged up the beach stern first. Here they were propped up with poles or stones. Like all galleys these ships also had masts and sails. The mast, which was made from fir, was slotted into a box fitted to the keel of the ship. The square sail could only be used when the wind was in the right direction. When the ship was not in use the mast and rigging were taken from the ship and stored ashore.

Black ships

Homer most often refers to ships as black, but he occasionally describes them as red or blue painted. The black probably refers to the tarring of the keel. The parts of the ship above the water line could be of various colours.

Early vase paintings

The very stylized vase paintings of the 8th century BC often depict ships. These invariably show a curved stern like a scorpion's tail, a ram at the front and above the prow a great S-shaped horn. These same characteristics appear on an iron fire dog from the 8th-century grave at Argos (see p.36). This fire dog confirms that the prow horn is single not double. These ships are most certainly galleys rowed by men who faced the rear of the ship. Often thole pins can be seen in the paintings. The interpretation of these paintings is difficult but it is probable that the artist is showing both sides of the ship (see the fragment above on right).

Like those of the Mycenaean age these ships were steered by one or two stern oars and had a ram at the front.

The Athenians however refused to desert their relatives on the island.

Realizing that the Greek fleet was about to break up Themistocles, the wily Athenian politician, sent a message to the Persian king. He told him that the Greeks planned to withdraw. Xerxes immediately split his fleet to guard both entrances to the channel. One-third sailed across to the western entrance whilst the rest moved up during the night to the eastern approaches.

At dawn the Greeks saw the Persian fleet drawn up in line of battle. They knew that they had to fight. In haste they despatched a few ships to stop the Persians coming up the western end of the channel. They then pulled the rest of their ships down to the water and climbed aboard. To the rhythmic chant of their war song they pulled at their long oars and moved out in column across the channel.

Xerxes took up his position on a hillside overlooking the strait. When the Greek line had moved right out into the channel the triremes turned to face the mighty Persian fleet. As if overwhelmed by the sight of their enemy the Greek line wavered and the ships in the centre began to back water.

◀ Fragment of an early vase painting. It shows both sides of a galley. The hook-shaped projections in the square openings are thole pins with straps.

▲ A bireme in rough sea, from a 6th-century vase painting. It has a ram in the shape of a boar's head. The crew are furling the sail.

Biremes
The early vase paintings often show what appears to be two banks of oarsmen (see the lower picture left). The artist is probably trying to show the rowers on both sides of the ship. The bireme (two-banked galley) was probably developed at the end of the 8th century by the Phoenicians and later adopted by the Greeks. The largest Greek galley of this period still had only 50 oars (*pentekonter*).

The Athenian navy
After the collapse of the Mycenaean civilization the Phoenicians became the major sea power. Later the Phoenician fleets became the mainstay of the Persian navy. After the first Persian invasion (490 BC) Athens became involved in a naval war with Aegina in which she was beaten. This insult to her pride prompted her to turn to the building of a fleet.

When the Persians invaded again in 480 BC although Athens could not match the experience of the Phoenician seamen, she could put to sea a navy of 200 of the latest style triremes (see p.44). This was more than all the other Greek states combined.

The vast amount of timber needed for the building and maintaining of this fleet caused the deforestation of central Greece and soil erosion was noticeable as early as Plato's day (early 4th century).

The harbour at Piraeus
The new fleet needed a more secure anchorage. Originally the Athenians had beached their ships at Phalerum. After the Persian retreat they fortified the rocky promontory of Piraeus with its three natural harbours (see p.48). They built moles to narrow the harbour entrances so that they could be closed with chains. The harbours were connected to the city by long walls which ensured access at all times.

The Battle of Salamis

The battle in the straits

The Phoenician and eastern Greek ships which made up the main part of the Persian fleet now began to move into the channel between the island of Salamis and the mainland. When they saw the Greek line falter and begin to retreat they raised a great shout and charged. Confident in their belief that the Greeks would turn and flee they strained on their oars and headed for the centre of the Greek line. In the middle the Greek ships continued to back water drawing the Persian fleet deeper and deeper into the crescent of ships. Still the Persians came on until the whole fleet

had entered the channel.

Then the trap was sprung. The trumpets blasted and on both wings the Greeks attacked: the triremes crashed into the Persian vessels in a devastating flank attack driving the Persians towards the centre of the strait.

The Persian ships were crammed together in uncontrollable confusion in the middle of the channel. They were unable to move as the Greek vessels darted in, their underwater rams smashing through the banks of oars and into the unarmoured sides of their ships. The Persian seamen fought bravely under the watchful eye of their king, but their plight was hopeless. In the confusion of the battle the Persians rammed and sank some of their own ships. Above the creaking of the timbers and the splintering of oars could be heard the groaning of the seamen crushed beneath the decks.

The Athenian sailors showed no mercy to the foreigners who had burned their beloved city. Grabbing oars or any other weapon that came to hand they brutally clubbed to death or drowned the shipwrecked Persians as they struggled helplessly in the water.

▼ The battle of Salamis. The Persian fleet is caught in the narrow straits where the superior seamanship of the Phoenician crews was of no use.

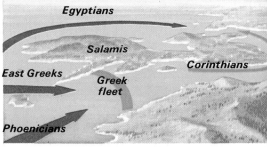

The battle of Salamis

On the evening before the battle the combined Greek fleet was beached behind the narrow finger of land that stretches out from the island of Salamis towards Athens. The fleet consisted of about 300 triremes and seven *pentekonters*.

To the south lay the Persian fleet of about 1,000 galleys—mainly triremes. About half of these were Phoenician, the rest being Egyptian and eastern Greek.

The Egyptian fleet was sent to bottle up the western end of the channel while the rest closed the eastern end. The Greeks despatched their Corinthian squadron to keep the Egyptians away.

The exact position and line-up of the battle is uncertain. As the channel is only about 1,600 metres wide and each trireme would need at least 20 metres in which to manoeuvre, the Greek fleet must have been drawn up at least four deep. The Athenians occupied the position of honour on the right wing.

The Greek vessels formed up in a straight line across the channel and turned their rams towards the Persians. As the Persians advanced the Greek centre backed water to draw them further into the strait. When the Greek wings charged, the Phoenician seamen, crammed in the narrow strait, were unable to use their superior skill. They were fighting in unfamiliar waters whereas the Greeks knew every sandbank and reef.

The Trireme

The Spartan revenge

Realizing they had sailed into a trap the Persians managed to withdraw what remained of their battered fleet. Among the dead was Xerxes' own brother. Although the Greeks had severely mauled the Persian navy their victory was incomplete. But the great king had lost his confidence. Leaving Mardonius in command, Xerxes withdrew to Asia with a large part of his army. Mardonius retreated into Thessaly and went into winter quarters with an army of about 120,000 men.

In the early summer of 479 BC the Spartan king,

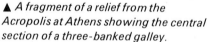

▲ A fragment of a relief from the Acropolis at Athens showing the central section of a three-banked galley.

The trireme

Sometime during the 6th century a third bank of rowers was added to the bireme to produce the famous trireme. By the end of the century the trireme had become the standard warship of the Mediterranean.

There is still a great deal of controversy surrounding the trireme but certain factors are clear. It was rowed at three levels with one man to each oar. From the pictorial evidence it is abundantly clear that the trireme was rowed at three levels. A chance remark by Thucydides— "It was decided that each sailor taking his oar, cushion and oarstrap..." proves there was one man to each oar. We learn from Athenian naval records that these oars were between 4 and 4.5 metres long. Athenian ship sheds at Piraeus have been excavated. These give maximum dimensions for the ships, that is, 37 metres long, 3 metres wide at the bottom, increasing to about 6 metres at outrigger level.

The rowers

According to Athenian records there were 27 rowers each side at the lowest level (thalamite). These rowers worked their oars through ports. Although these were not far above water level they must have been sufficiently high for light rowing boats to slip underneath for this is what the Syracusans did to attack the Athenian rowers at their benches. There were 27 rowers in the second bank (zygite).

The top bank (thranite) rowed through an outrigger. This was an extension beyond the side of the ship which gave greater leverage to the oars. There were 31 thranite rowers on each side. As in previous eras the ships were steered by broad oars at the rear.

▲ The stern of a trireme from an Etruscan bronze casket.

Pausanias, at the head of a Greek army of about 50,000 hoplites and 60,000 light-armed troops, advanced into central Greece.

The two armies encamped near Plataea. The Greeks attempted to change their position under cover of night, but at dawn the line had not been reformed. The Spartans hastily formed up on the right wing but the Athenians had failed to reach their new position leaving a gaping hole in the Greek line.

Mardonius saw this golden opportunity and led the whole of his Persian forces against the Spartan right wing leaving his allies to deal with the rest of the Greeks. The Spartans crouched behind their shields as they were showered with missiles. Behind them on the hillside Pausanias offered sacrifices but the omens were unfavourable. Stung by the hail of missiles some of Sparta's allies broke ranks and charged the enemy. Unable to hold his men back any longer Pausanias ordered the attack. The Spartans rose as a man and charged. Mardonius himself was struck down in the middle of the fray, and with him fell most of his thousand-strong bodyguard. The Persians fled the field. Pausanias had avenged Leonidas and gained Greece's finest victory.

▼ *Reconstruction of a trireme—side and plan view. Scale 1:65.*
▶ *Section through same vessel showing rowing positions.*
▶▶ *Coins showing:* **1**. *The front of a galley c. 480 BC;* **2**. *The front of a later galley with reinforced bows.*

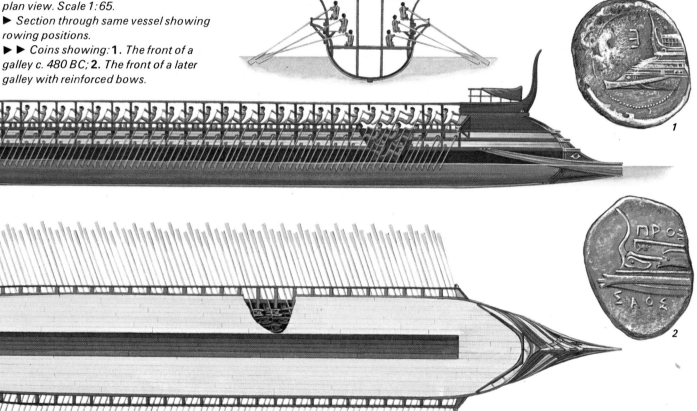

Crews

The crew of a trireme was 200 of whom 170 were rowers. These were drawn from the poorer classes. They were not slaves. At the battle of Salamis each ship had ten marines and four archers. The crew also included a flautist who piped time for the rowers. This left fifteen deck hands. The ship was commanded by a *trierarch* who was appointed by the general.

Armament

The main weapon was the bronze-plated ram at the front. To use this required great manoeuvring skill. During the war with Sparta the Corinthians reinforced their bows and the outrigger and crashed their ships into the Athenian vessels, thus replacing skill with brute force. There is little evidence for grappling hooks and other boarding equipment.

Speed

Over long distances and under favourable conditions a trireme could hope to average 9 kilometres per hour. There are numerous examples of long distances being covered at more than 8 kilometres per hour. Aeneas the tactician recommends ships as the quickest method of military transport. To estimate a trireme's greatest speed is impossible. The fastest speed for a rowing eight over 2,000 metres is just over 20 kilometres per hour. The trireme's speed must be well below this, possibly 12 to 15 kilometres per hour.

Later Galleys

After the battle of Plataea both Athens and Sparta were free to pursue their empire building which the Persians had interrupted. Although both states followed an anti-Persian policy and openly supported any anti-Persian activities in the eastern Mediterranean, it was only a matter of time before they were at each other's throats.

For half a century an intermittent peace existed between the two states. In order to fight the Persians at sea the Athenians formed a league of the maritime states. This was known as the Confederacy of Delos.

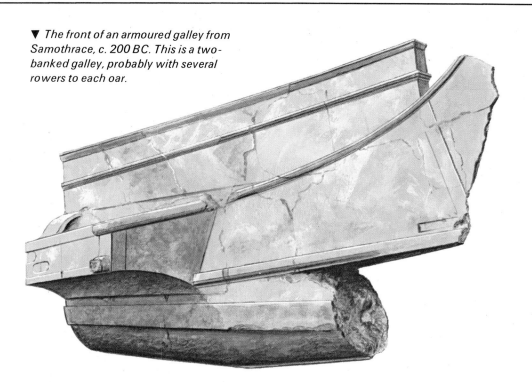

▼ *The front of an armoured galley from Samothrace, c. 200 BC. This is a two-banked galley, probably with several rowers to each oar.*

1. *Front of a Hellenistic galley, c. 300 BC.*
2. *Front of a Carthaginian galley, c. 220 BC.*

The confederacy of Delos

After the defeat of the Persians Athens formed a league with the maritime states of the Aegean. This alliance was called the Confederacy of Delos. Each state contributed ships, or, more often, money to continue the war against Persia. The net result was that Athens built up a great fleet at the expense of the other members of the Confederacy. By 420 BC her fleet reached 350 vessels.

The Athenians' control of the sea lasted for 75 years. During the war with Sparta (431–404 BC) the Corinthians' reinforced bows caused great damage to the lighter Athenian ships but still they retained their superiority. Athens' final humiliating defeat at Aegospotamoi (405 BC) was not caused by lack of skill but sheer carelessness. When Athens finally fell the Spartans confiscated all except twelve of her triremes.

Armament

The Greek ships which fought at Salamis were almost unarmed. They were only partially decked and, if the representations are not misleading, the rowing benches of at least the upper bank were protected only by the decking above. There was no railing along the sides of the deck: this was presumably to make boarding easier.

By the end of the 5th century rowers must have had more protection as the Syracusans had to get in under the oars in order to attack the Athenian rowers through the oar holes.

In the Macedonian era (after 320 BC) the function of the galley changed. Ships were designed as heavily armoured floating platforms to carry either catapults or marines. These ships were fully decked and their sides were completely blocked in (see sculpture above).

The fleets of Philip and Alexander

During the first part of the 4th century Athens regained her naval supremacy but it was short lived. When Philip II of Macedon smashed the combined armies of the Greeks, Athens had no alternative but to surrender. From 337 BC her fleet came under the control of Philip and his successors. Soon after, when Alexander the Great broke the hold of the Persians in the eastern Mediterranean, the whole Persian fleet went over to his side. But peace at sea did not last long. When Alexander died in 323 BC his generals divided the empire, army and fleet amongst themselves.

By exercising more and more control over her fellow members in this league, Athens managed to convert a partnership into an empire. With the money appropriated from her allies she built a great fleet and the great city that was the wonder of all the ancient world.

In 431 BC the long expected war broke out. At first it seemed that neither side could possibly win for Athens controlled the sea and Sparta the land. Sparta could lay siege to Athens but could not stop supplies coming in from the sea. On the other hand Athens could launch seaborne attacks on southern Greece but could not defeat the Spartan army. It became a war of sieges without one full-scale land battle. From the beginning Athens suffered from ill luck. When the Spartans besieged the city, food was brought in from Egypt. But these same ships also brought the plague. In the crowded conditions of the siege Athens was devastated by the disease. But the irony was that because the Athenian navy was operating a blockade against Sparta the Spartans themselves never contracted the disease. For three years the plague raged and killed about a quarter of the population.

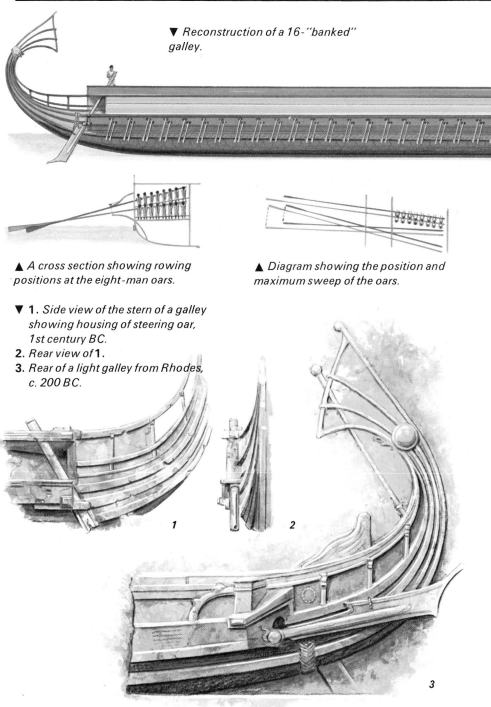

▼ *Reconstruction of a 16-"banked" galley.*

▲ *A cross section showing rowing positions at the eight-man oars.*

▲ *Diagram showing the position and maximum sweep of the oars.*

▼ 1. *Side view of the stern of a galley showing housing of steering oar, 1st century BC.*
2. *Rear view of 1.*
3. *Rear of a light galley from Rhodes, c. 200 BC.*

The naval arms race
About 400 BC we first hear of galleys larger than the trireme. The Greek word for a three-banked galley was *triereis*. Now there appears a *tetrereis* and a *pentereis*, that is, four and five "banked". Sixes appear about 350 BC and by the end of the century eights, nines, tens, elevens and thirteens. Early in the 3rd century there is a sixteen and by the end of that century a colossal forty "banker".

The reconstruction of a heavy-weight
This multiplication of banks of oars has mystified scholars for centuries and will no doubt continue to do so. It is impossible that these galleys had ever-increasing banks of oars. In probability no ship ever had more than three banks. This is certainly the largest number shown in Greek and Roman art. It seems probable that these figures refer to the number of men rowing each vertical group of oars. So a four was probably a doubled-up bireme and a five a trireme with one man at the lowest oar and two at each of the upper oars. In the 17th and 18th centuries it was found that eight was the maximum number of men that could handle a single oar. On the trireme system a twenty-four is therefore conceivable. Beyond this point there must have been some further reorganization. The most mentioned of these giants is the sixteen. This is most acceptable as a bireme (two banker) with eight-man oars. The reconstruction above is based on this conclusion.

Fortified Towns

Athens invades Sicily

The war between Athens and Sparta resulted in a stalemate. After the defeat of Persia the Athenians had massively strengthened the defences of their city. Provided that the long walls connecting Athens to Piraeus remained intact and food could be brought in by sea, it was impossible for Sparta to overcome her opponent. In 421 BC a peace treaty was signed which left Athens hardly worse off than she had started.

In 416 BC, still lusting for empire, Athens embarked on the most disastrous blunder in Greek history—she decided to invade Sicily. This culmi-

Athens and her harbours

1. *Main harbour Kantharos.*
2. *Inner harbour.*
3. *Zea harbour.*
4. *Munychia harbour.*
5. *Salamis battle strait.*

Town walls

Very little advance was made in military architecture during the five hundred years that followed the collapse of Mycenaean civilization. The citadel or acropolis was still the focal point of the defences of towns down to the end of the 7th century. Only in the 6th century were serious attempts made to fortify whole towns. Under pressure at first from Lydia and then Persia the eastern Greeks were compelled to improve their method of fortification.

When tracing out the walls to encompass a town there was a tendency to try to make use of natural defences such as cliffs or steep slopes. This often meant increasing the area of the town. These walls were usually pierced with narrow sally ports which enabled the defenders to launch attacks on the besiegers outside the walls.

Earlier walls were constructed of rubble masonry or even mud. Now carefully cut rectangular or polygonal blocks of stone were used. Mud brick probably continued in use for battlements.

Towers

The main innovation was the use of projecting towers. At first these were only used at weak points and at gateways. By the 5th century regularly spaced two-storey towers were normal. These towers enabled the defenders to pour down a greater concentration of missiles on their attackers.

Long walls

After the retreat of the Persians, Athens set about rebuilding her walls. It was essential to Athens that she secured communications with her new harbour at Piraeus. To do this the Athenians built a massive wall round Piraeus and linked the harbour with the town by two long walls fortified at intervals by two-storey towers. These long walls enclosed a corridor about 100 metres wide by 6,500 metres long.

This system was copied by other Greek states. However, although this type of defence was effective against Sparta, it would hardly have withstood a concentrated Persian siege.

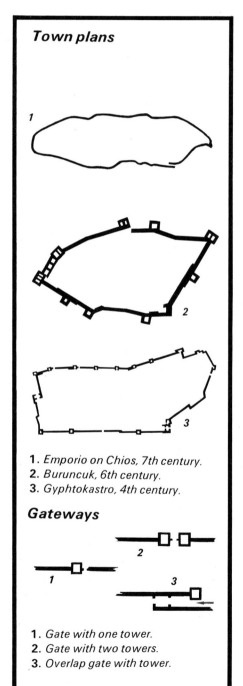

Town plans

1. *Emporio on Chios, 7th century.*
2. *Buruncuk, 6th century.*
3. *Gyphtokastro, 4th century.*

Gateways

1. *Gate with one tower.*
2. *Gate with two towers.*
3. *Overlap gate with tower.*

48

nated in the siege of Syracuse. It should have been easily accomplished but, owing to the incompetence and indecision of the general Nicias, turned into an unmitigated disaster.

At first the people of Syracuse did not believe that their city was the chief aim of the Athenian expedition and therefore took no precautions.

The Athenians made a brilliant start, drawing the Syracusan cavalry northwards whilst they sailed southwards for a seaborne invasion. But in spite of a victory in the battle that followed Nicias failed to exploit his success and withdrew.

It was not until the next summer that Nicias again approached Syracuse. In preparation for the expected Athenian assault the Syracusans arranged a review of their troops. The parade was to take place in the plain south of the Epipolae plateau. Nicias heard of the review. The night before it was due to take place he embarked his troops and sailed southwards.

Once again the Athenians made a brilliant start: they landed their army just north of the plateau and while the parade was taking place to the south stormed the hill.

▲ Reconstructed view of the Athenian frontier fort at Gyphtokastro. Its walls are reinforced by regularly spaced two-storey towers.

Frontier forts

During the late 5th and early 4th centuries Athens built a series of frontier fortresses. These fortresses were built to secure communications and as a precaution against attack.

The fortress of Eleutherae at Gyphtokastro is a typical Athenian frontier fort. It was built to crown a steep-sided hillock guarding the road from Athens to Thebes. It has walls two metres thick faced with rectangular blocks of grey stone. The walls are fortified with a series of two-storeyed towers projecting inwards and outwards from the walls. The towers were entered from the town by a door at the street level. A second door at first-floor level led out on to the battlements. In the earlier part of the 4th century the towers would have had flat platforms with crenellations at the top. The battlements could be approached by steps from street level.

▶ A reconstructed tower from Gyphtokastro.

Gateways

Very little advance was made in gateway design before the 4th century. The old Mycenaean types with modifications remained in use. There was the overlap type often defended with a tower at the end of the outside wall. This form was usually designed to expose the enemy's unshielded right side. There was also the type cut straight through the walls. This was usually defended by one or two towers or bastions.

The gates were made of heavy timber and closed by a bar. This bar was locked in place by a cylindrical pin which was dropped into a hole in the bar locking the bar to the jamb. The pin disappeared below the top of the bar and could not be removed without a key.

▼ A bar and lock from the Lion Gate at Miletos. The bar **A** is pulled across from its channel in opposite wall **B**. It is slotted into hole **C**. The locking bar **D** is fitted over **A** and slotted into hole **E**. The lock pin **F** is pushed down locking the two bars together.

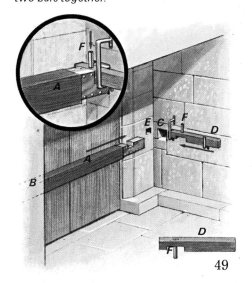

49

Siege Tactics

Syracuse is besieged

With staggering speed the Athenians began to build the double lines of circumvallation around Syracuse. On the plateau they erected two forts—Labdalum to cover the northern approaches, and the round fort to cover the southern.

At first the Syracusans tried to impede the work with their cavalry. When this failed they built a counterwall across the line of the Athenian walls. Nicias mounted a surprise attack and, catching the Syracusans off guard, captured their wall.

The Athenians dismantled the Syracusan wall and

Siege tactics

In siege tactics the Greeks lagged far behind the Persians. The use of tunnels (mines) to collapse enemy walls and mounds which enabled the attackers to get up to the level of the walls, were the primary siege weapons of the Persians. The battering ram had been in use in Asia for centuries. In Greece however there is no evidence of any of these tactics before the second half of the 5th century. Even then the main siege tactic of the Greeks was the blockade.

The mound

During the war with Athens a Spartan army laid siege to Athens' ancient ally Plataea. Thucydides gives a vivid description of this siege. Initially the Spartans erected a stockade, then a mound.

First they constructed two containing walls of timber laid like lattice work (see illustration). This type of timber wall can be seen being used by the Romans on Trajan's Column. Next they filled the space between these timber walls with rubble, earth and wood. From this mound they hoped to attack the battlements.

The Plataeans countered by heightening the wall with bricks held together by a wooden framework. This was covered with hides to protect the workmen. They also dug under the walls and began removing the earth from beneath the mound. Fearing that this was not enough, they constructed a wall behind the wall that was under attack.

Battering rams

The Spartans now brought up battering rams (see p. 66). The Plataeans countered by lowering nooses over the battlements and pulling the rams up. They also hung great beams over the battlements suspended from poles by two chains. These were dropped on the ram to break off the head.

Siege walls

When attempts to fire the city had also failed the Spartans reverted to the usual Greek and Roman tactic. They built a wall around the town to starve it out.

First two ditches were dug about eight metres apart. A double wall of mud brick was built between these ditches. This left a space about five metres wide between the walls. This was roofed over to form a sentry walk above and living quarters below. The sentry walk was fortified with battlements on either side. At intervals of about 15 metres two-storey towers were built.

The Athenians at Syracuse seem to have been building a similar double wall but it was never completed. This wall was constructed of wood and stone.

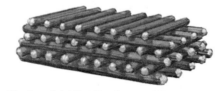

▲ Timbers laid like "lattice work" to make the containing walls for mounds.

The Athenian siege of Syracuse

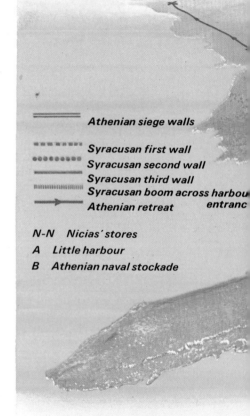

═══════	Athenian siege walls
▬ ▬ ▬ ▬	Syracusan first wall
●●●●●●●●	Syracusan second wall
▬▬▬▬▬	Syracusan third wall
▭▭▭▭▭▭▭	Syracusan boom across harbour
➤	Athenian retreat

Syracusan boom across harbour entrance

N-N Nicias' stores
A Little harbour
B Athenian naval stockade

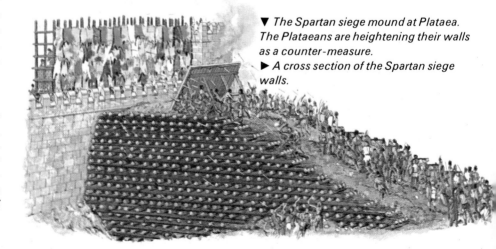

▼ The Spartan siege mound at Plataea. The Plataeans are heightening their walls as a counter-measure.
▶ A cross section of the Spartan siege walls.

used the material to continue their own wall southwards. Again the Syracusans tried to stop them, this time with a ditch and palisade across the marshes at the edge of the great harbour. Again the Athenians attacked. Carrying doors and planks they advanced across the marshes to the palisade. In the battle, although the Syracusans were defeated, one of the Athenian generals was killed. The Syracusans retired behind their walls.

The blockade was complete. Syracuse must fall—it was a matter of time. But Nicias, in an incredible act of stupidity, left the Epipolae end of the wall unfinished. He thought the Syracusans would surrender.

Syracuse appealed to Sparta. The Spartans refused to send an army but did send a general, Gylippus. The Spartan general landed in northern Sicily. Here he managed to collect about 3,000 irregular troops and advanced on the beleaguered city. He was prepared to fight but to his astonishment he was not opposed and under cover of night climbed the Epipolae hill and entered Syracuse. From this moment nothing went right; the gods themselves seemed to have turned against the Athenians.

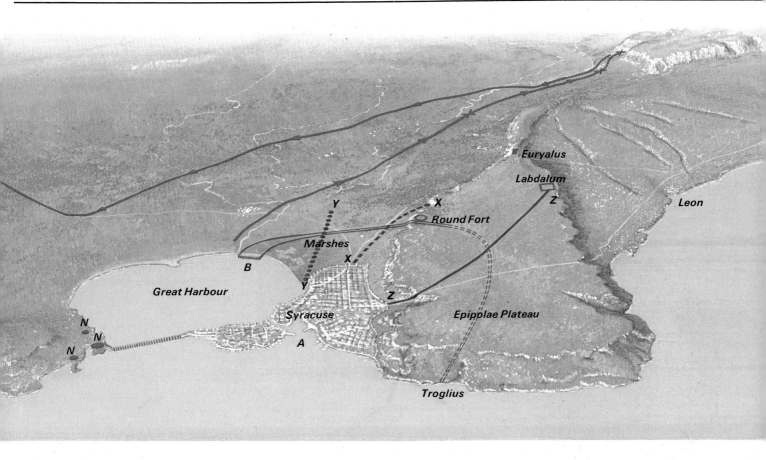

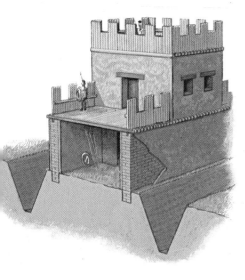

The siege of Syracuse

When Nicias captured the Epipolae plateau his first job was to secure the north and south ascents. To do this he built two forts: the Labdalum and the round fort. From the round fort the Athenians began constructing their blockade wall which was to extend north and east to the sea at Trogilus. In order to cut off the southern extension of this wall into the plain the Syracusans built a counter wall (**XX**). When the Athenians captured this a second attempt at counter-works was made. This second line (**YY**) consisted of a ditch and palisade extending across the marshes. This was also taken and the Athenians completed their southern line. This wall was double. The two walls diverged at their south end to contain the naval base which was also protected by piles driven into the harbour bed.

Gylippus accepted the Athenian southern lines as impregnable. He therefore launched his attack on the uncompleted wall on the plateau. He captured Labdalum and managed to build a counter-wall (**ZZ**) from the town to the fort, making the completion of the Athenian lines impossible.

Auxiliaries and Mercenaries

Gylippus assumes command

Gylippus immediately took over command in Syracuse. He captured the Labdalum fort in a surprise attack and constructed a wall along the hilltop, making it impossible for the Athenians to complete their wall.

Nicias wrote home asking Athens to call off the siege. Athens responded by sending reinforcements. Sparta, in order to detain these reinforcements, reopened the war in Greece.

Up till now the Syracusans had not used their considerable navy because of the reputation of the

Archers and slingers

It was not until the late 5th century that the Greeks began to realize that the phalanx was not the ultimate weapon. Athens had long employed archers and slingers who were drawn from foreign lands where these primitive weapons were still used. Scythian archers had been in use since the 6th century. Scythian bows had a range of about 150 metres. Cretan archers were also very popular. Many arrow heads have been found varying in size and shape from the very large Cretan type (**10**) to the tiny Scythian type (**8**).

1. *A plate from northern Italy showing a hoplite stringing a Scythian bow.*
2. *The Greek view of a Scythian archer from a plate in the British Museum. Compare with the Scythian version on page 23.*
3 and 4. *A Cretan bow and arrow from a Greek vase.*
5. *A reconstruction of a Scythian bowman.*
6. *A small gold medal of a bowcase from a Scythian grave.*
7-10. *Various types of arrowheads from Greek sites (British Museum). Scale 1:2.*

Peltasts

Of all the light-armed troops the peltast was the most effective. He was named after his wicker shield (*pelta*). According to Aristotle it was rimless and covered with goat or sheep skin. Aristotle seems to imply that it was round. In art it is shown as crescent shaped. The *pelta* is sometimes shown with a single handgrip and sometimes with the double hoplite-type grip. The *pelta* also had a strap for carrying. Xenophon gives a very amusing description of peltasts climbing fences with their shields on their backs getting caught up and hanging by their shield straps. The peltast was of Thracian origin and wore the traditional costume of his country—patterned cloak, high boots and fox-skin cap with ear flaps. He wore no armour. His weapons were javelins. These troops were employed for the first time during the Sparta–Athens war.

These light-armed forces had always been treated as inferior troops, used only for skirmishing. But in 390 BC a young Athenian general, Iphicrates, with a highly trained and disciplined group of Thracian peltasts, annihilated a Spartan *mora*. This feat completely changed the Greek attitude to peltasts and ensured Iphicrates a place in military history. In 349 BC Athens even sent an army against Philip of Macedon that was composed entirely of peltasts and a small body of cavalry.

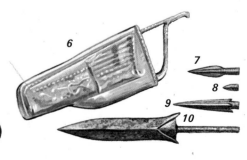

Athenian fleet since Salamis. Now they launched a combined land and sea attack on the Athenian store bases at the southern end of the great harbour. Although the Syracusan navy was repulsed, the supply bases were captured. The Athenians were in a desperate position. The Syracusan ships retired to their base and here a strengthening modification was carried out to their bows (see p.45).

Gylippus was determined there should be a decisive encounter before Athenian reinforcements could arrive. He advanced in full force against the Athenians but this was a cover for the main attack which was against the Athenian fleet. The surprise failed and Nicias managed to deploy his ships for a defensive battle. The Syracusans failed again, but in a third attempt two days later they managed to draw the Athenians into a full-scale battle in which, with their reinforced bows, they crashed straight into the Athenian galleys causing devastation. The myth of Athenian naval invincibility was dispelled for ever.

At this point the Athenian reinforcements of about 15,000 men and 73 triremes sailed into the great harbour. The force included much needed light-armed troops and cavalry.

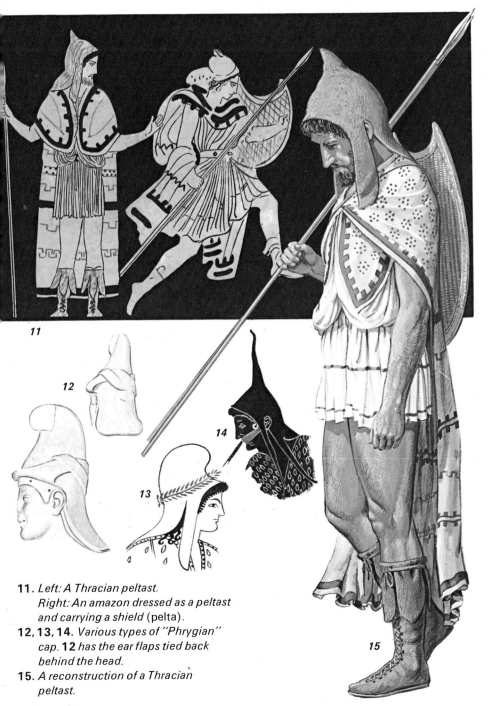

11. Left: A Thracian peltast.
Right: An amazon dressed as a peltast and carrying a shield (pelta).
12, 13, 14. Various types of "Phrygian" cap. 12 has the ear flaps tied back behind the head.
15. A reconstruction of a Thracian peltast.

Slingers

Slingers were much used from the mid-5th century onwards. The men of Rhodes were the best. The most effective sling shot was of lead.

◀ A lead sling shot with the inscription "take that".

Mercenaries

Our earliest accounts of Greek soldiers serving as mercenaries come from Egypt in the 7th–6th centuries. They are found also serving as bodyguards to the early Greek tyrants during the same period. With the rise of Persia many Greeks found service with Persian governors first as bodyguards and later as shock troops.

The employment of hired soldiers within Greece only really began during the war between Sparta and Athens. During this war both sides employed mercenaries of one sort or another.

At the end of this long war many soldiers who had known no other life but soldiering offered their services for hire. Xenophon was one of the 10,000 such men who accompanied Cyrus in his attempt to usurp the Persian throne. The hiring of mercenary troops both inside and outside Greece became common during this period. The situation became so bad in Greece that mercenary commanders were even prepared to march their troops against their own towns.

When Alexander invaded Persia he was opposed at all three of his great battles by Greek mercenary infantry. In fact the Persian king placed so much reliance on these men that he handed over the defence of Turkey to their commander. Alexander slaughtered these "traitors" to his Greek ideal without mercy.

Marching, Camping and Baggage

Disaster for Athens

Demosthenes, the leader of the reinforcements, took command and immediately launched a night attack with the whole force on the Epipolae Hill. The attack was repulsed with massive losses. Demosthenes wanted to raise the siege but Nicias now refused to move.

For another month the Athenians remained. Disease now decimated the army. When reinforcements began to arrive in Syracuse, Nicias could justify staying no longer. But it was too late.

The Syracusans launched a naval attack and drove

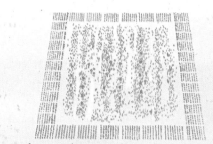

▲ *An army in square formation. Individual units are marching eight abreast.*

▼ *The same army advancing through a narrow pass: the units vary their width according to the narrowness of the road.*

The hollow square

When Nicias withdrew from Syracuse his army marched in a hollow square with the baggage and camp followers in the middle. This was the normal Greek method of marching under attack.

At the end of the 5th century BC a Greek army penetrated deep into the Persian empire in an attempt to place Cyrus the Younger on the Persian throne. The attempt failed and an army of 10,000 Greeks was forced to make a tactical retreat. This retreat, 1,300 kilometres up the Tigris and over the mountains of Armenia to the Black Sea, is recorded by Xenophon. In his account he gives us a marvellous description of the hollow square in practice.

The army is divided into four parts. Two divisions marching in column form the flanks and the other two parts marching in phalanx form the front and rear of the square. All the light-armed, the baggage and non-combatants are in the centre.

Each *lochos* is drawn up so that it can march either in file where the road is narrow or several abreast in open country. This shows the practical use of drill (see p.30). This exercise allowed whole *lochoi* to fall back when necessary so that the square could contract or expand.

Normal marching

When advancing through open country the baggage train was at the front covered by a screen of cavalry or light-armed troops. The phalanx brought up the rear hurrying on the stragglers. When passing through a narrow pass the phalanx marched in column on either side of the baggage train. Each part of the army was responsible for its own baggage. If attacked on the march the army could deploy to either flank. Each *lochos* would wheel in column to face the threat.

▲ *An army advancing through a defile under normal conditions. The baggage train is in the centre and the phalanx in column on either side. At the bottom the column is forming into phalanx (see page 31) to meet an attack.*

the Athenian fleet back to the shore. They then chained a row of ships across the harbour sealing the Athenians within the bay.

In desperation the Athenian fleet tried to break out but in the attempt they lost nearly half their ships. The decision was made to abandon the fleet and retreat by land. The Athenians set out marching in a hollow square. For days the army blundered on continually assailed by the Syracusan cavalry and light-armed troops. Finding the route impassable the Athenians turned south, marching through the night. But the next morning the Syracusan cavalry caught up with them. Finally the two generals surrendered with the shattered remnants of their troops. Of the nearly 50,000 men who had set out to conquer Syracuse only 7,000 remained. The Syracusans executed Nicias and Demosthenes. The rest of the army were shut up in the quarries where many died, the survivors being later sold into slavery.

In spite of this staggering loss of an entire army and 175 ships, Athens continued the struggle against Sparta for another nine years. In the end the rest of her fleet was captured and Athens herself was besieged. In the face of starvation Athens surrendered.

Camping

The Greeks were never as conscious as the Romans of the value of a fortified camp. Xenophon tells us that the Spartan camp was round which could imply a perimeter of a ditch or fence. The only really detailed account that we have of an army on the march is Xenophon's retreat of the ten thousand. In this account, although the army is basically Spartan, and in spite of the constant threat of an enemy attack, no attempt is made to fortify a camp. It was only when a long-term occupation was intended that a ditch and stockade were constructed.

It is amusing to note that the Spartans feared a slave revolt so much that it was considered more important to guard the arms than the perimeter of the camp. As Plutarch remarks "they feared more from their friends than their enemies."

◄ Hoplites and an archer preparing to go on campaign. One is putting his shield in its leather cover—from a Greek vase found in Italy.

The baggage train

When a Spartan army set out it was very well equipped as one would expect. Baggage was carried either by pack animals or waggons. Each pack animal carried an axe and sickle and each waggon a shovel and pick. Besides the soldiers' equipment the baggage train would carry medical supplies, timber for running repairs to the waggons and all the tools that might be needed.

◄ A pack donkey (British Museum).

Provisions

If a campaign was expected to last at least fifteen days, each man had to take twenty days' rations with him. This was carried by a servant. Rations consisted of barley or wheat, cheese, onions, wine and various salt foods.

In Athens and the other city states similar systems existed for both baggage and provisions though they were seldom as efficient. If a hoplite did not have a servant he carried his supplies in a haversack on his back. The army was accompanied by pioneers to clear the way for the waggons and also smiths, carpenters and leather workers. These were all non-combatants.

▼ A donkey with wood-framed pack.

The Age of Alexander

The age of Spartan domination did not last long. Iphicrates and his peltasts had shown that a Spartan army could be beaten. It only required a general of genius to destroy the myth completely. Thebes found two such generals: Epaminondas and Pelopidas. These two produced a revolutionary concept of hoplite tactics. In the summer of 371 BC Sparta invaded Theban territory. At Leuctra she came face to face with the Theban army and was decisively defeated. The Thebans in turn invaded southern Greece and at the great battle of Mantinea in 362 BC, confirmed that the days of Spartan supremacy were over.

The whole course of Greek history was changed when in 359 BC a 23-year-old youth called Philip became king of Macedon in northern Greece. Eight years previously he had been taken as a hostage to Thebes where he met Epaminondas and Pelopidas. Their revolutionary military ideas were not wasted on Philip. On his accession to the throne he set about building up the most formidable fighting machine the world had yet seen. It was with that machine that his son, Alexander the Great, was to conquer an empire that stretched from Egypt to India.

After his death Alexander's empire was divided amongst his generals. These kingdoms lasted until one by one they were swallowed up by Rome.

Our evidence for this period is vast, spread over an area from Spain to Mesopotamia. Samples of armour have been found from Spain to the Euphrates. Artistic evidence comes from as far afield as Alexandria, Tyre and Pompeii. The literary evidence includes treatises on tactics, catapults, towers, rams and even drill manuals.

◄ *The beginning of the greatest career of conquest in history: Alexander leads his cavalry across the Granicus river to attack the Persian army.*

The Macedonian Phalanx

Philip invades Greece

The main strength of the Macedonian army had always been the cavalry. When Philip came to the throne in 359 BC he immediately set about the re-organization of the inferior infantry. During the next years Philip established his control over the country north of Greece from the Adriatic to the Black Sea. The Greek states were too busy fighting amongst themselves to notice the giant shadow stretching southwards. There was one voice alone that spoke out against Philip: that of Demosthenes, but his warnings went unheeded.

▼ *A* syntagma *(256 men), the smallest tactical unit of the Macedonian phalanx. The hoplites are drawn up in close order sixteen deep. The pikes of the first five ranks protrude beyond the front.*

The Theban tactic

The Thebans were the first to see the weakness of the phalanx. As long as it was opposed by another phalanx face to face the Spartan army was unbeatable. But what would happen if enormous pressure were brought to bear on just one point? At the battle of Leuctra (371 BC) the Thebans deepened one wing of the phalanx. The result was shattering. The Spartan wing crumbled under the pressure and the rest of the line fell to pieces.

The Macedonian phalanx

This brute-force breakthrough formation which was adopted and developed by the Macedonians demanded the use of the pike or two-handed spear. The Macedonian pike (*sarissa*) was between 5.5 and 6.5 metres long. In a charge the spears of the first four or five ranks projected beyond the front line; the rest held their spears up in the air to break the impact of missiles. When attacked the phalanx could take up a defensive formation (locked shields) with a file every half metre.

The composition of the phalanx

A Macedonian drill manual has been preserved by Asclepiodotus (1st century BC). Although late, it in no way contradicts the account of Polybius (c. 203-120 BC).

The ideal phalanx is made up of 64 battalions. Each battalion (*syntagma*) contains 256 men and is commanded by a *syntagmatarch* (see right). It was made up of 16 files (*lochoi*) each of 16 men. Each front-rank man (*lochagos*) commanded his file. His second-in-command was the rear-rank man (*ouragos*). There was also a half-file leader (*hemilochites*): if the phalanx was to be drawn up eight deep he would move up next to the *lochagos* with his half file behind him. Similarly there was a quarter-file leader (*enomotarch*).

Files were coupled in pairs commanded by a *dilochites* who would be the right-hand file leader. Similarly two pairs were commanded by a *tetrarch* and four by a *taxiarch*.

Thirty-two battalions formed a wing (*keras*) commanded by a *kerarch*. The complete phalanx of two wings was commanded by a *strategos*.

Drill

On the parade ground close order and locked shields are formed from open order by commanding the end file to stand fast while the other files turn towards them and close up. They then face the front and the ranks close up in the same way. In the face of the enemy half and quarter files must move up as in Spartan drill (see p.31). This was called doubling. It could be done sideways with ranks. This movement could be used to open or close ranks and made it possible to double or halve the depth or width of the phalanx.

To form up facing the rear three methods of counter-marching were used:
1. The Spartan (see p.31). This is equivalent to a retreat.
2. The file turns about. The *ouragos* stays put whilst the rest of the unit marches past him. This is more formidable because the phalanx advances.
3. The file turns about and everybody changes places. In this case there is no movement of the phalanx.

Drill orders must be given in a clear voice stating the direction before the command, for example, right turn, not turn right.

In the autumn of 339 BC Philip took advantage of this chaos and moved into central Greece. At last the Athenians took notice. Demosthenes was sent to Thebes to patch up an alliance. The next summer, at Chaeronea, Thebes and Athens met Philip in battle. Philip commanded on the right wing. His young son Alexander, who was eighteen, commanded the left, which was composed of the best troops. According to plan Philip allowed the Athenians to push his troops back, thus drawing them on to unfavourable ground. Alexander smashed into the Theban line. The cream of the Theban army was slaughtered.

Then Philip attacked on the right wing. The Athenians, who were over-confident, thinking they were victorious, broke ranks and fled. The centre of the allied force was now caught and crushed between the two Macedonian wings.

Philip offered far more lenient terms of peace than Athens expected and they were accepted. Philip felt no such generosity towards Thebes. He had expected them to join with him against Athens. The Theban leaders were executed or banished. The prisoners were sold into slavery and a garrison occupied the citadel.

The composition of the syntagma

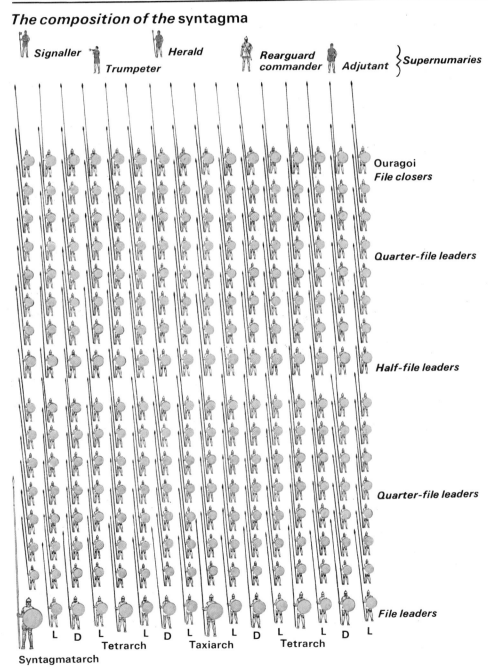

Signaller
Herald
Trumpeter
Rearguard commander
Adjutant
} Supernumaries

Ouragoi
File closers

Quarter-file leaders

Half-file leaders

Quarter-file leaders

File leaders

L   D   L   D   L   D   L   D   L
Tetrarch   Taxiarch   Tetrarch

Syntagmatarch

L = Lochagos
D = Dilochites

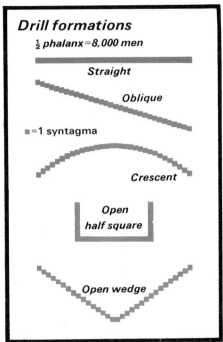

Drill formations
½ phalanx = 8,000 men

Straight

Oblique

■ = 1 syntagma

Crescent

Open half square

Open wedge

Battle order
There were now many variations to the straight front formation of the 5th century. There was oblique formation with either flank advanced. There were crescent, half-hollow square or hollow-wedge formations, all with flanks either advanced or retarded. Marching was practised in all these formations as well as in column of varying depths.

Marching
On campaign the baggage train was always in the position farthest from the enemy. If attack were threatened from the front the baggage should be in the rear. Likewise the baggage train would be on the right of the phalanx if attack were expected from the left. If attack were expected from all sides the army would form a hollow square as in the previous period.

Armour and Weapons

Alexander crosses to Asia

All the states of Greece, with the exception of Sparta, now agreed terms with Philip. At the congress of Corinth a Greek confederacy was set up with Philip as its leader.

Philip announced his intention of attacking Persia and the necessary forces were requisitioned. Before the enterprise could be realized Philip was assassinated and Alexander came to the throne. He was twenty years old.

On Philip's death the Greeks defected. Alexander's reaction was so fast that he reconquered Greece with-

Helmets

The Thracian helmet was the most popular type in early Macedonian times c. 350–250. One may be seen on the Alexander sarcophagus at Istanbul. Fourth-century Thracian helmets often have cheek pieces in the form of a beard and moustache. The Chalcidian and Attic helmets continued in use. A conical helmet, possibly of Celtic origin (4), was also very popular in the 4th century.

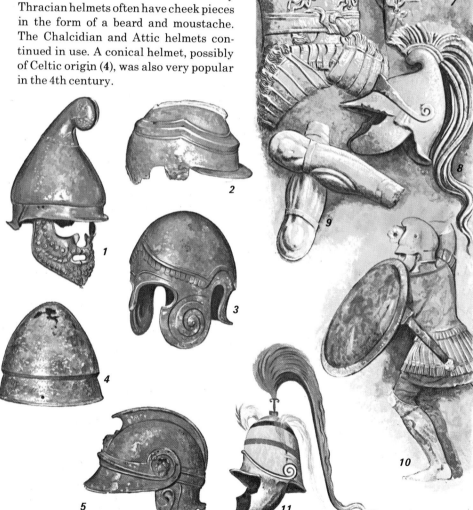

▲ 1-4. Fourth-century helmets.
1. Thracian; 2. Thraco–Attic type;
3. Chalcidian; 4. Bell type.
5. Later Thracian type, c. 150 BC.
6-9. Armour shown on the reliefs from Pergamon, Turkey.

6. Short muscled cuirass; 7. Linen cuirass;
8. Thracian helmet; 9. Strap on greaves.
10. An infantryman from the Alexander sarcophagus.
11. Helmet from a Macedonian tomb painting.

Body armour

In his *Life of Alexander* Arrian often refers to the light-armed part of the phalanx. There is also a fragment of a late 3rd-century inscription from Amphipolis which seems to confirm this. This inscription records the fines imposed for the loss of military equipment. The fine imposed on a file leader for the loss of a cuirass is twice that imposed on other ranks. It seems likely that front-rank men wore metal-plated cuirasses or short-muscled cuirasses, and that the other ranks wore linen ones. It is possible that in Alexander's time rear rankers wore no body armour at all.

Greaves

Greaves are listed on the Amphipolis inscription and shown in art. Those on the reliefs from Pergamon in Turkey are held on by straps in the Italian style.

The shield

The Macedonian shield has caused much confusion. Plutarch, describing the Macedonians at the battle of Pydna (168 BC), says that their shields were hung on their left shoulders and when they advanced they brought them round to the front. The Macedonian shield is rimless. This type of shield was adopted as it was impossible to use a two-handed spear while holding the hoplite shield. The Aemilius Paullus monument at Delphi shows the inside of such a shield (see right 4). It has a hoplite-style grip. Experiments show that it can be used very efficiently using only the arm band and controlling the angle by the neck strap. When a hoplite shield is being carried, the inside of the rim (7) fits comfortably over the left shoulder taking the weight off the arm. It is the absence of this ridge on the rimless type that made a carrying strap necessary. This strap would also have taken much of the weight of the great spear.

out striking a blow. Then he turned to the north and west, crushing all opposition. During these campaigns he was reported dead and Greece again revolted. Alexander marched south and again the Greeks surrendered without a blow—all that is except Thebes. Alexander took the city and razed it to the ground.

In the spring of 334 Alexander crossed the Dardanelles at the head of a combined Macedonian–Greek army of 30,000 infantry and 5,000 cavalry. The infantry was composed of 12,000 Macedonians who made up the phalanx. A further 12,000 were hoplites and peltasts supplied by the Greek states. The remaining 6,000 were light-armed javelin men (*agrianes*), Cretan archers and Thracian peltasts. The cavalry were made up of the Macedonian "companions" 2,000 strong, 1,800 Thessalians and squadrons of Greek, Paeonian and Thracian horsemen.

While the army crossed the Dardanelles Alexander sailed for Troy. He was the new Achilles—the champion of the Greeks. As Achilles had done a thousand years before, Alexander sacrificed in the temple of Athena. He brought back with him the sacred shield that was to save his life.

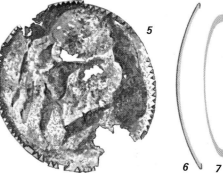

1 *and* **2.** *Shields from a Macedonian tomb.*
3. *Shields from the relief at Pergamon.*
4. *Inside of a shield from the Aemilius Paullus monument at Delphi.*
5. *Remains of a bronze shield from Pergamon. Scale 1:15.*
6. *Suggested restored section of* **5.**
7. *Section of a hoplite shield for comparison.*

Swords

Although the normal hoplite sword continued in use, the most popular sword in this period was the *kopis*. This is a single-edged slashing weapon with a curved blade. This sword was introduced into Greece in the late 6th century but appears in Italy as early as the 8th century. It gradually eclipsed the hoplite sword. Some examples have been found in Spain.

The spear

The Macedonian spear (*sarissa*) was a long pike held in both hands. There is much controversy about the length of this weapon. Most ancient writers suggest it was about 5.5 metres long. But Polybius, who is a very reliable source, states that in his day (2nd century BC) it was about 6.5 metres long. He goes on to say that in the past it had been almost a metre longer. Polybius must be accepted for the later measure but the earlier one has to be doubted. He also tells us that the *sarissa* had a counter-weighted butt —probably a heavy shoe.

1. *A curved sword of Greek type from Spain. Scale 1:6.*
2. *Handle of Greek sword of same type.*
3. *The two types of sword from a Macedonian tomb painting.*
4. *Spear butt from the reliefs at Pergamon.*
5. *A spearhead from Vergina in Macedon. Scale 1:6.*

Cavalry: Development and Equipment

The first blood

The Persians were determined to stop Alexander's campaign before it started. At the Granicus river the Persian cavalry was drawn up in line, with a phalanx of Greek mercenaries behind. Alexander advanced with his infantry in the centre and the cavalry on the wings. In true Theban style he had strengthened one wing—which he himself led. The opening attack came from this wing.

Alexander, at the head of his bodyguard the Companions, charged into the muddy river and up the bank the other side. The charge was so violent that

Early cavalry

There is no evidence for the tactical use of cavalry in southern Greece before the 5th century BC. It is true that cavalry was used in early times in the Thessalian plain, but in the south the mountainous terrain was unsuitable. There is no mention of Greek cavalry during the Persian wars. By the time of the war between Sparta and Athens, cavalry was in regular use, however it was only used for skirmishing. The Athenians also employed mounted archers. They were usually of Scythian origin.

Our main knowledge of cavalry during this period comes from Xenophon. He recommends that the cavalryman wears a cuirass with protection for the thighs, a guard for the left arm and a Boeotian helmet with all-round vision. The thigh protection was probably the *pteryges* (see p.38). The left armguard, used in the absence of a shield, seems only to have been in vogue in his own day. He suggests a bronze chest plate (peytral) and face guard (chamfron) for the horse. He also prefers the curved *kopis* (see p.61) to the straight sword and javelins to spears.

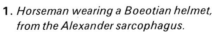
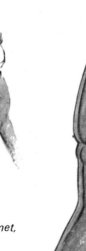

1. *Horseman wearing a Boeotian helmet, from the Alexander sarcophagus.*
2. *Boeotian helmet (Ashmolean Museum).*
3. *Helmet of similar type (Ashmolean Museum).*
4. *Crested chamfron, lamellar peytral, masked helmet and armguards shown on the relief from Pergamon, c. 230 BC.*
5. *Bronze peytral (Naples Museum).*
6. *Chamfron (Karlsruhe Museum).*
7. *Horses wearing blankets and a primitive saddle, from a Macedonian tomb painting.*

▲ *A full-length muscled cuirass made very broad at the hips to enable its wearer to sit on a horse.*

they crashed through the Persian wing.

The Persians launched a counter offensive under the command of Mithridates, the son-in-law of the Persian king. Alexander rode straight for Mithridates to intercept this movement. The Persian hurled a javelin at Alexander which would have killed him but for the sacred shield from Troy. The javelin merely pierced his shield and stuck in his linen cuirass. Alexander pulled it out and charged forward. His spear struck Mithridates on the chest but splintered. Unhurt Mithridates now drew his sword and closed for the kill. In desperation Alexander thrust his broken spear into his enemy's face, knocking him from his horse.

In the confusion a Persian horseman struck Alexander a blow with his sabre that cut right through his helmet. Alexander fell from his horse and the Companions crowded round him.

In the meantime, as the Persian wing began to waver, more Macedonian units managed to cross the river until the whole army was over. The Persian cavalry broke and fled. Alexander had recovered enough to order his men to attack the Greek mercenaries to whom he showed no mercy.

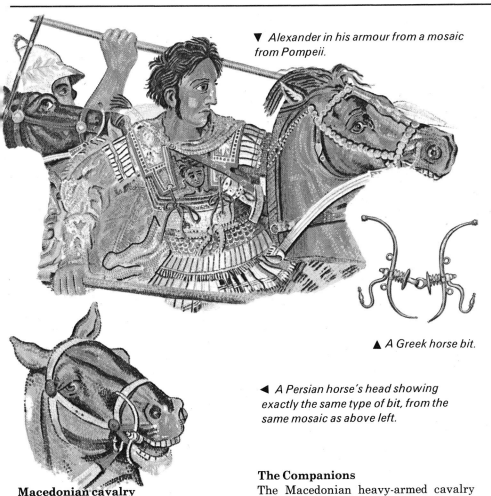

▼ *Alexander in his armour from a mosaic from Pompeii.*

▲ *A Greek horse bit.*

◄ *A Persian horse's head showing exactly the same type of bit, from the same mosaic as above left.*

Cavalry formations

A = Unit commander
B = Wing commander
C = Rearguard commander

Greek

Thessalian

Macedonian

Macedonian cavalry

Alexander put a greater emphasis on cavalry than the Greeks ever had. He used his cavalry for direct frontal assaults. Although there is insufficient information to be able to describe Alexander's cavalry, it must have been heavily armed. Cavalrymen certainly carried heavy spears, but shields are uncertain. Thessalian cavalry of Alexander's time and later Macedonian cavalry were certainly heavy armed carrying a long spear and a round shield.

Alexander introduced mounted archers and javelineers into his army. These were also used in later times.

The Companions

The Macedonian heavy-armed cavalry had developed from the king's mounted bodyguard: the Companions. By the time of Alexander the bodyguard had grown to eight squadrons—about 1,700 men. During his Asiatic campaign Alexander reorganized his whole cavalry into five *hipparchies* each with one unit of Companions. He retained one over-size squadron of 300 Companions as his bodyguard. The *hipparchy* became the standard unit of the Macedonian cavalry. Asclepiodotus divides the *hipparchy* into eight squadrons (*ilai*) each commanded by an *ilarch*. His ideal army has two cavalry wings each of four *hipparchies*.

Formations

Greek cavalry had usually formed up in a square with the files much closer than the ranks, that is, sixteen horsemen wide and eight deep. The Thessalians developed a diamond formation which charged point forward to break through the enemy line. This formation was modified by the Macedonians into a triangular formation but used for the same purpose. In both the diamond and triangular formations the commander would be posted at the foremost point.

63

Catapults, Moles, Ramps and Mines

The siege of Tyre

The following year was spent in the conquering of Asia Minor (Turkey). The Persian king Darius moved northwards with a large army and Alexander advanced to meet him. The two armies came face to face at Issus near the border of Turkey and Syria. Again Alexander's cavalry smashed through the Persian archers and light-armed infantry. Darius did not wait to see the outcome of the battle but fled in his chariot. Although at first the Persian army fought bravely, the news of the king's flight dampened their ardour and they too turned and fled.

The revival of siege techniques

No advance had been made in siege warfare since the great days of the Persians in the 6th century BC. But at the turn of the 5th to 4th century great improvements were made in both siege and counter-siege techniques. The new advances took place not in Persia or Greece but in Sicily.

When the Persians invaded Greece the Carthaginians had made a simultaneous and equally vain effort to conquer Sicily.

Soon after the destruction of the Athenian army at Syracuse the Carthaginians again tried to take over the island. The Carthaginians had revived and improved the ancient siege craft. They built huge moveable towers higher than the walls of the towns they besieged. From these they raked the battlements with missiles to clear them of defenders. At the same time they used rams against the walls.

These new methods made the countermeasures used at Plataea impossible (see p.50). For a while it looked as if all Sicily would fall to the invaders.

A=Stock
B=Slider
C=Trigger mechanism

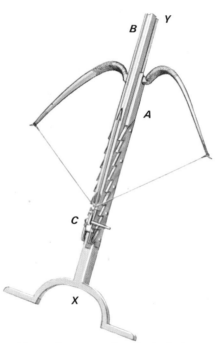

▲ *The earliest catapult—the belly bow (gastraphetes). The bow was drawn by putting the stomach at* **X** *and* **Y** *on the ground and using the weight of the body to force back the slider* **B**.

The invention of the catapult

At Syracuse a young man called Dionysius seized power. He fought the Carthaginians at their own games, adopting and improving their techniques. But he went one further. His engineers invented the arrow-shooting catapult. This machine, and the stone-throwing version that was developed from it, came to dominate siege warfare both for attack and defence. Both Philip and Alexander used them extensively. At first these machines were no more than oversize crossbows. By the time of Philip a torsion type had been developed, powered by twisted sinew. This later type could be adapted for stone throwing. In 332, when Alexander besieged Tyre, he was able to shake the walls of the town with huge stones.

Before the end of the century a Macedonian general, quite justly known as Demetrius "the besieger", built massive machines capable of throwing rocks weighing about 80 kilograms. The heavy stone-throwers probably had a range of about 150 metres. With his stone-throwing machines Demetrius was able to strip battlements from walls.

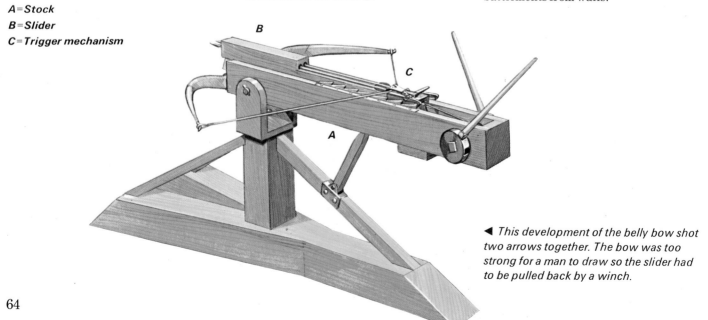

◀ *This development of the belly bow shot two arrows together. The bow was too strong for a man to draw so the slider had to be pulled back by a winch.*

Alexander decided to try to gain control of the coast before advancing eastwards. In this way he hoped to cut off the Persians from their Mediterranean fleet.

As Alexander advanced southwards through Phoenicia (Lebanon) the ancient cities of Sidon and Byblus surrendered. But Tyre, which was situated on an island about 800 metres from the coast, refused him entry. The Tyrians had once withstood an Assyrian siege lasting 13 years. They thought that Alexander stood no chance of taking their city without naval supremacy.

Alexander began to build a mole out towards the island. As the advancing causeway came within range of the Tyrian artillery he moved two siege towers armed with catapults up to the end of it. These kept up a constant barrage on the walls of the city. The Tyrians prepared a fire ship which they weighted down at the stern to raise the bows out of the water. They managed to beach this on the end of the mole and so fire the siege towers. Assaulted by a constant hail of missiles from the Tyrian warships, Alexander was forced to withdraw and watch his siege towers burn.

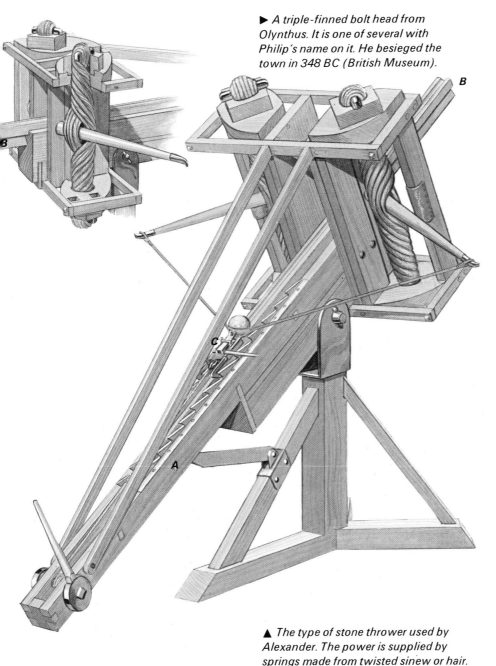

▶ A triple-finned bolt head from Olynthus. It is one of several with Philip's name on it. He besieged the town in 348 BC (British Museum).

▲ The type of stone thrower used by Alexander. The power is supplied by springs made from twisted sinew or hair. The inset above left is cut away to show the spring.

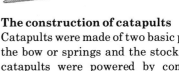

The construction of catapults

Catapults were made of two basic parts— the bow or springs and the stock. Early catapults were powered by composite bows, the later type by springs of hair or sinew which were tightened by twisting. The stock, **A**, had a slider, **B**, which moved along it. This slider had a trigger mechanism, **C**, which gripped the bow string. The slider was pulled back drawing the bow string with it. When it was fully drawn the arrow or stone shot was inserted. Then the trigger was released and the missile was shot along the top of the slider. To reload the slider was pushed forward until the trigger mechanism could be hooked to the string again. Vitruvius gives dimensions for machines throwing stones of up to 120 kilograms.

Moles and ramps

Moles and ramps were the natural development of the mounds of the classical period. Their construction was basically the same as the earlier mounds. Their purpose was to move siege towers and other machinery up to the walls. The channel between Tyre and the mainland was not deep. The Macedonians drove piles into the mud to hold the mole together. The causeway itself was made of stones and packed down with timber and mud.

Mines

Another Persian siege device adopted by the Carthaginians and Macedonians was the use of mines. This involved burrowing tunnels under walls. These tunnels were supported by wooden props. When the wall was sufficiently undermined the props were fired and the mines caved in bringing down the wall with them.

Towers, Rams and Drills

The Persian fleet joins Alexander

Just when Tyre seemed unassailable Alexander had an almost unbelievable stroke of luck. The Persian fleet was composed mainly of Phoenician ships. When the crews heard that most of Phoenicia had surrendered, the fleet disintegrated and the Phoenician squadrons offered their services to Alexander.

Now the control of the sea was in his grasp, Alexander set about widening the mole. He built new machines, some of which were rolled out on to the widened mole and others placed on ships lashed together in pairs.

Towers

Dionysius of Syracuse built moveable towers six storeys high for his siege of the Carthaginian port of Motya (398 BC). He probably filled these with his newly invented artillery. This was certainly what Alexander did when he besieged Tyre.

Vitruvius the Roman military engineer quoting Alexander's engineer Diades, tells of towers up to an incredible 60 metres high. However, 30-metre towers seem to be more normal. Diades describes a 30-metre tower as 8 metres wide at the base and tapering to 6.5 metres at the top. The four upright beams around which it was constructed were 20 centimetres wide at the bottom tapering to about 14 centimetres at the top. The tower was divided into ten storeys each with windows on three sides. At each floor level was a balcony 1.5 metres wide. The whole tower was covered with raw hides. These towers were moved on wheels or rollers. Diades managed to construct these towers so that they could be dismantled and carried with the army.

Shortly after the death of Alexander, Demetrius "the besieger" built an enormous tower 40 metres high. It had nine storeys, into which he crammed catapults of varying sizes. On the lowest floor he placed his giant 80-kilogram stone-thrower. At each successive stage he placed smaller machines. On the top floor he had his light arrow shooters—Scorpions. This tower had iron armour plating on three sides.

▶ The great iron-clad tower of Demetrius "the besieger". It was 40 metres high and divided into nine storeys crammed with catapults of varying sizes.

Rams and drills

The battering ram developed rapidly in the 4th century. By Macedonian times huge ram-bearing vehicles known as tortoises had been developed. Vitruvius, again quoting Diades, describes some of these machines. The tortoise ram had a housing 16 metres long and 10 metres high with a low pitch roof. On top of this was a tower two metres square and about 10 metres high. It was divided into three storeys. The lower two held pots of water for extinguishing fires. The top floor contained a small catapult.

Inside the housing the ram itself moved on rollers. It was pulled backwards and forwards on ropes. Earlier rams had been suspended by ropes from the central beam of the housing. Being operated like a pendulum these early suspension rams had a limited stroke with a decreasing momentum at the point of impact. Roller rams had a constant momentum and much greater penetration. The housing of these machines was covered with planks of oak or some other low combustion wood. On top of this was a layer of green wattle. The whole housing was covered with seaweed or straw soaked in vinegar sandwiched between two layers of oxhide.

Vitruvius also describes a drill or borer. This moved on rollers along a wooden trough and was operated by a windlass and pulleys. Whereas the ram's job was to shake down walls the drill was used to knock a hole through a wall.

The Tyrians retaliated by raising towers on their battlements and by dropping boulders into the shallow water near the walls to prevent the ships coming close.

Meanwhile squadrons from the disintegrated Persian fleet continued to join Alexander. The fleets from Rhodes, Turkey and Cyprus now joined the siege. In a surprise attack the Tyrians rowed out of the harbour and attacked the Cypriot squadron while the crews were at lunch. Several of the vessels were destroyed. But Alexander, in a lightning counter-attack captured two of the Tyrian ships as they were re-entering the harbour.

The Macedonians now launched an all-out assault. The ships with the rams and towers were brought up and part of the walls demolished. Further ships with boarding bridges moved in and two sections of the wall were taken. The Phoenician and Cypriot fleet now forced its way into the harbour. Under this combined attack the city fell. Eight thousand Tyrian men were killed in the onslaught. Alexander showed little mercy and many of the men, women and children were sold into slavery. The siege had lasted seven months.

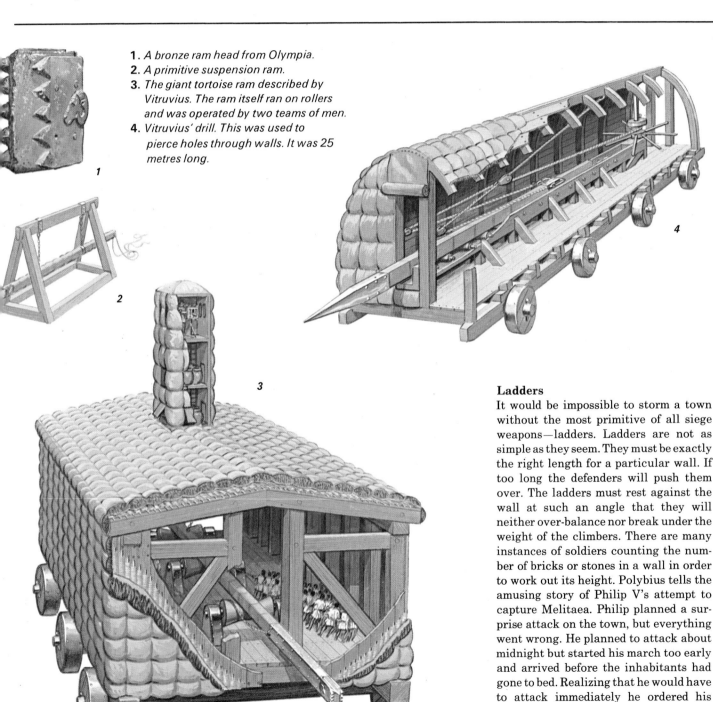

1. A bronze ram head from Olympia.
2. A primitive suspension ram.
3. The giant tortoise ram described by Vitruvius. The ram itself ran on rollers and was operated by two teams of men.
4. Vitruvius' drill. This was used to pierce holes through walls. It was 25 metres long.

Ladders

It would be impossible to storm a town without the most primitive of all siege weapons—ladders. Ladders are not as simple as they seem. They must be exactly the right length for a particular wall. If too long the defenders will push them over. The ladders must rest against the wall at such an angle that they will neither over-balance nor break under the weight of the climbers. There are many instances of soldiers counting the number of bricks or stones in a wall in order to work out its height. Polybius tells the amusing story of Philip V's attempt to capture Melitaea. Philip planned a surprise attack on the town, but everything went wrong. He planned to attack about midnight but started his march too early and arrived before the inhabitants had gone to bed. Realizing that he would have to attack immediately he ordered his ladder bearers forward, only to find that his ladders were too short!

Fortifications

Darius flees again

Alexander advanced on Egypt, which was quick to surrender. On the coast he established the city of Alexandria. This is only one of the many fortified towns which he founded, many of which bear his name to this day. He now returned to Syria. From Syria the Macedonian army marched eastwards crossing the Euphrates and the Tigris. Darius had had a year and a half to collect together a new army. The "great king" moved up the Tigris to oppose Alexander at Gaugamela. The Persians had brought scythed chariots with them, which they hoped would

Artillery for defence

With the introduction of more sophisticated siege techniques it was soon realized that if the enemy managed to get up to the city walls defence was hopeless. The modifications that took place in the 4th and 3rd centuries BC were mainly concerned with keeping the enemy at a distance.

Artillery could be used for defence as well as offence. From the middle of the 4th century walls and towers were designed to hold artillery. Both were pierced with loop holes and artillery ports. The towers were often four to five storeys high. A tilt roof replaced the old open battlements. These towers had heavy artillery at second floor level and lighter at the top. The higher the artillery the greater was its range.

The towers had postern gates from which sallies could be made against the enemy. Again the purpose was to keep the attackers from the walls.

Outworks

A large ditch or series of ditches was dug in front of the walls. These kept the heavy artillery, towers and rams out of range. The outer ditches were usually protected by palisades and thorn hedges. The inner one was protected by stone outworks behind which were artillery emplacements. Beyond these ditches were covered holes and artificial marshes to trap the machines.

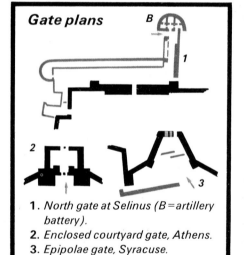

Gate plans

1. North gate at Selinus (B = artillery battery).
2. Enclosed courtyard gate, Athens.
3. Epipolae gate, Syracuse. Outworks are marked in red.

▲ Vaulted wall compartments with loopholes at Perge. Inset: section of a loophole.

▶ A tower with loopholes and shuttered windows for catapults (Paestum, Italy).

The city walls

The city walls themselves were thickened and heightened. The old crenellated battlements were done away with and replaced with screen walls with shuttered artillery ports and loopholes. Vaulted rooms reminiscent of Tiryns were built into the walls for the troops' quarters. At Carthage even elephants were stabled in the walls.

breach the phalanx.

Alexander placed his javelineers well out in front to break up the chariot charge. As usual he commanded the right wing, which advanced to make the first assault. The scythed chariots charged but most were soon put out of action by the javelineers. The phalanx opened and let the remaining chariots pass through. Before the infantry lines met Alexander had gained the upper hand on the right wing. The Persian infantry were now subjected to a combined cavalry and infantry attack. The line broke and once again Darius fled.

On the left the Persians were much more successful and managed to break through the phalanx. Alexander brought up reinforcements, but before he could get across the Persians heard of their king's desertion, lost heart and fled.

Alexander now marched on Babylon which surrendered. Susa and Persepolis also fell to him. Hearing that Darius was at Hamadan Alexander hastened northwards. Once more the Persian king fled. Riding day and night Alexander pursued him. Just southeast of the Caspian Sea he caught up, but the "great king" was dead—he had been killed by his bodyguard.

185 metres

▲ *The original plan of the Euryalus defences.*

◄ *The great battery at Euryalus, Syracuse, with the Epipolae gate in the background. An underground passageway ran from the left side of the gate to the battery.*

Archimedes and Syracuse

In the 3rd century BC there was a man living in Syracuse who is claimed to be the greatest engineer of the ancient world. This man, Archimedes, set about improving the fortifications of his town.

When the Romans besieged Syracuse (211 BC) they were terrified by his "science fiction" machines. These dropped enormous stones on their ships or lifted them out of the water.

The Romans moved right up to the walls under cover of night, believing that they were moving "inside" the range of Archimedes' machines. At dawn machines began shooting arrows through slits at every level of the wall.

The Euryalus fort

Archimedes' greatest achievement is probably the fortification of Euryalus at the westernmost tip of the Epipolae plateau (see p.51). Archimedes designed a massive catapult battery to defend this approach to the plateau. This consisted of five solid stone pylons about 11 metres high. On these he mounted huge stone-throwing catapults. From this elevated position these machines could out-range anything that the enemy could produce. In front of the great battery were three ditches. The furthest at a distance of about 185 metres was at the maximum range of his elevated artillery. An enemy would have to cross this under fire while out of range with their own catapults.

Gates

The most common form of gate in this period is the courtyard type. This involved indenting the line of the walls to form a courtyard in front of the gate. Often this would be enclosed with a second gate at the outer end. The Epipolae gate at Syracuse is of the open courtyard type but later its front was closed by a series of outworks.

War Elephants

The last battle
Alexander's ambition was now fulfilled but his restless spirit would not let him stop. He continued his march eastwards, fighting battles and founding cities. He heard of opposition in the north and turned in this direction. He passed Samarkand and pushed on into Russia to the end of the known world. Here he established another town called Alexandria the Farthest. He then retraced his steps southwards and went into winter quarters at Balkh. The army had been campaigning unceasingly for two years and was very tired.

▼ *Representations of elephants with towers.*
1. *from Naples;* 2. *from Villa Giulia, Rome.*
3. *from The Hermitage, Leningrad.*
4. *A Carthaginian coin showing an African elephant.*

Elephants
At the battle of Gaugamela, 331 BC, the Persian army was reinforced by fifteen elephants. This was the first appearance of elephants in military history. When Alexander reached India five years later he was opposed by an army which included 200 of these brutes.

The European had been introduced to elephants now and for better or for worse every self-respecting army had to have them. For over a hundred years they were the great gimmick, in fact they were so valuable that Alexander traded the province of India for them. In 280 BC Alexander's cousin Pyrrhus invaded Italy and introduced the Romans to these living tanks. The elephants so far described are the Indian type. However it was not long before the African elephant was being used by the Egyptians and Carthaginians.

African and Indian elephants
Polybius the Greek historian, in describing a battle between Syria and Egypt, mentioned that the Indian elephant was larger than the African. This has caused much controversy for the reverse is true. It is now clear that the elephants described by Polybius were the forest type which is now extinct in North Africa. This species measured about 2.35 metres at the shoulder whereas the Indian measures just under three metres and the African bush type about 3.5 metres.

Although the Indians who opposed Alexander did not use towers on their elephants, the Indian elephant was large enough to be fitted with one. Towers were first used by Pyrrhus against the Romans in 280 BC. The North African forest elephant was too small to carry a tower. It was ridden like a horse.

Hannibal
In 218 BC the elephant reached the height of its fame when Hannibal took an army and about 37 elephants across the Alps to invade Italy. This was in late autumn at a period when all the passes were covered with snow all the year round. It was a fruitless exercise for by the spring of the next year only one elephant was still alive. The heyday of the elephant was the 3rd century BC; after this they fell out of favour.

It is interesting that the three greatest generals of antiquity—Hannibal, Pyrrhus and Alexander were all fascinated by elephants.

In the early summer of 327 BC the army crossed the western spur of the Himalayas known as Hindu Kush and descended into the valley of the Indus. Here Alexander was opposed by an Indian army with 200 elephants. The Macedonians won the ensuing battle but with terrible losses. After the battle Alexander set out for the conquest of India, but his army refused to go any further. It was clear that the soldiers had had enough. Reluctantly he turned south towards the coast and from there returned to Babylon. Two years later he was dead, leaving his generals to squabble over his empire.

Uses of elephants

Although the Indians used elephants against Alexander's infantry and the Carthaginians also used them in this way, their main use was against cavalry. Untrained horses were frightened by their smell quite apart from their size. Horses had to be trained specially to operate alongside them.

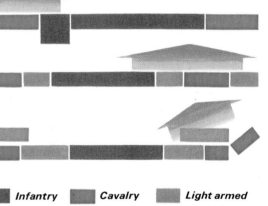

Infantry	Cavalry	Light armed

| Elephants | | First attack |

▲ Battle formations 5th–3rd century BC.
1. Marathon, 490 BC. **2**. Leuctra, 371 BC.
3. Issus, 333 BC. **4**. Raphia, 217 BC.

The changing face of battles

Many changes had taken place since the Persian wars of the 5th century. The phalanx which had once represented the total Greek armament was now only one part of the battle line-up. On the wings were various types of light-armed troops, cavalry and elephants. The first attack which used to come along the whole length of the line now usually came on one wing and often the phalanx was only involved in the final stages of the battle.

After the battle

After a victory trophies (displays of captured armour) were set up by the victors. Often both sides set up trophies. Pieces of armour were inscribed and dedicated in the sanctuaries. During the Macedonian period these inscriptions were usually made on shields. Examples of these trophies have been found at Olympia.

▲ Reconstruction of an Indian war elephant as used by the Macedonians in the 3rd century BC.

Alexander
Reaches India

The battle of the Hydaspes
▼ *Alexander's troops are confronted by an Indian army with 200 elephants. While the light-armed troops attack the elephants with axes and scimitars, the phalanx advances with locked shields driving the giant beasts back on to their own soldiers.*

Glossary

Some words are in their Greek form and others in their more common latinized form. In some cases the form that makes pronunciation easiest has been used. The plural form is given after the Greek nouns.

agrianes light-armed Macedonian troops.

Attic helmet a helmet derived from the Corinthian type of helmet, but with ear holes and no noseguard.

baldric a shoulder strap for carrying a sword.

bastion a solid stone tower projecting from a wall.

battlements the defences along the top of walls.

bireme a galley rowed at two levels.

Boeotian helmet a cavalry helmet with a broad brim.

bronze age name given to the era when bronze was the main metal used for weapons and tools, in Greece c. 2000–1000 BC.

Chalcidian helmet helmet similar to the Attic type of helmet but with a nose guard.

chamfron face guard for a horse.

circumvallation the walls built around a town by a besieging army. Their aim was twofold: to stop anyone escaping and to stop help getting in.

cistern an underground source of water.

citadel a strongly fortified retreat.

classical period in Greece the period from c. 480–300 BC.

Corinthian helmet a face-covering helmet very popular in the 7th–6th century BC.

crenellations the indentations in battlements.

cuirass armour for the torso.

cyclopean the name given to the massive stones used to build bronze-age citadels —from Cyclops, the one-eyed mythical giants.

dark ages the period that succeeded the collapse of the Mycenaean civilization, c. 1100–800 BC.

dilochites Macedonian commander of two files.

dowel a wooden rod.

enomotarch in Sparta a file leader; in Macedon a quarter-file leader.

enomotia, enomotiae a file or a quarter of a Spartan *lochos.*

figure-eight shield a bronze-age shield shaped like an eight.

file a line of men from the front to back of the phalanx.

forecastle a raised platform at the front of a ship.

fresco a wall painting.

galley a warship propelled by oars.

greave a leg guard.

heavy-armed forces troops with full armour.

Hellenistic era c. 300–50 BC.

helot a Spartan slave.

hemilochites Macedonian half-file leader,

heroic term used to refer to period described by Homer in his poems.

hipparchy a Macedonian cavalry unit.

hippeis Spartan kings' bodyguard.

hoplite heavy-armed Greek infantryman.

ilai a subdivision of a *hipparchy.*

ilarch cavalry officer.

javelin throwing spear.

kerach commander of a *keras.*

keras half a Macedonian phalanx.

kopis a sword with a curved single-edged blade.

lamellar plates overlapping rectangular plates used as armour.

light-armed forces skirmishers who wore little or no armour.

linear B name given to Mycenaean writing.

lintel the horizontal support across the top of a doorway.

lochagos commander of a *lochos.*

lochos, lochoi smallest tactical unit in the Spartan phalanx. A file in the Macedonian phalanx.

marine a soldier serving on board a ship.

mine a tunnel.

mole a causeway.

mora one-sixth part of the Spartan army.

mound a pile of earth used to get up to the level of the battlements when besieging a town.

Mycenaean era name given to the great bronze-age civilization of mainland Greece.

ouragos the rear-rank man of a file.

paean battle song.

panoply complete battle dress.

pelta a crescent-shaped shield.

peltast a light infantryman armed with javelins and a *pelta.*

pentekonter a 50-oared galley or, pronounced *pentekonteer,* a commander of a *pentekostyes.*

pentekostyes half a Spartan *lochos.*

pentereis a galley with five banks of oars.

peytral chest armour for a horse.

phalanx Greek infantry formation made up of several ranks of spearmen.

pike a two-handled spear.

polemarch commander of a Spartan *mora.*

pteryges tongues of fabric for protection of the thighs, at the bottom of a cuirass.

rampart defensive wall of earth.

rank line of men from end to end of the phalanx.

sally port a narrow gateway in a city wall.

sarcophagus a stone coffin.

sarissa the long Macedonian pike.

scale armour armour made of overlapping metal plates like scales on a fish.

stern castle a raised platform at the rear end of a ship.

strategos a general.

syntagma the smallest tactical unit of the Macedonian phalanx, 256 men.

syntagmatarch commander of a *syntagma.*

tang a spike projecting from the metal part of a weapon—used for fixing it to the shaft or handle.

taxiarch commander of half a *syntagma.*

tetrarch commander of a quarter of a *syntagma.*

tetrareis a galley with four banks of oars.

thalamite the lowest level of rowers in a trireme.

thole pin a rowlock—a spike used for fixing the oar to the side of the boat.

Thracian helmet a peaked helmet not unlike the Attic helmet but it gave protection for the ears.

thranite the upper level of rowers in a trireme.

trierarch commander of a trireme.

triereis Greek for a trireme.

trireme a galley with three banks of oars.

zygite the middle level of rowers in a trireme.

People

Achilles the great champion of the Greeks in Homer's *Iliad.*

Aemilius Paullus Roman general who conquered Macedon 168 BC.

Aeneas ("the tactician") a 4th century Greek writer on tactics.

Agamemnon commander-in-chief of the Greek forces at the siege of Troy.

Alexander (the Great) King of Macedon and conqueror of Persia, d. 323 BC.

Archimedes the greatest mathematician—engineer of the ancient world, d. 212 BC.

Aristotle Greek philosopher, 384–322 BC.

Arrian Roman historian of the 2nd century AD. He wrote a life of Alexander the Great.

Asclepiodotus a Greek philosopher of the 1st century BC. He wrote a book on Macedonian military organization and drill.

Athena patron Goddess of Athens.

Carthaginians Phoenician colonists living at Carthage near Tunis on the north coast of Africa.

Companions name primarily given to the cavalry bodyguard of the Macedonian kings.

Cyrus the Younger Persian prince who led an army which included many Greeks against the King of Persia, 401 BC.

Darius (III) King of Persia who was defeated by Alexander, d. 330 BC.

Demetrius ("the besieger") King of Macedon remembered best for his siege tactics, d. 283 BC.

Demosthenes Athenian orator who spoke out against Philip II of Macedon, d. 322 BC.

Diades Greek military engineer in the service of Alexander the Great.

Dionysius (I) tyrant (dictator) of Syracuse, d. 367 BC.

Dorians a tribe of northern Greeks who invaded and settled in southern Greece in the 11th century BC.

Epaminondas Theban general who defeated the Spartans, d. 362 BC.

Gylippus Spartan general who led the Syracusan resistance during the Athenian siege.

Hannibal greatest Carthaginian general, who defeated the Romans in three great battles, d. 183 BC.

Hector Trojan champion in Homer's *Iliad.*

Herodotus 5th-century Greek historian who wrote a history of the Persian invasions of Greece.

Homer Greek poet who composed the two great poems, the *Iliad* and *Odyssey.* Everything about him is uncertain, even his authorship of the poems. He probably lived in the 8th century BC.

Immortals, the the Persian kings' bodyguard.

Iphicrates 415–353 BC, an Athenian general who defeated a Spartan *mora* with an army of peltasts.

Leonidas Spartan king who died at Thermopylae, 480 BC.

Mardonius Persian general killed at Plataea, 479 BC.

Mithridates Persian general who opposed Alexander at the battle of the Granicus, 334 BC.

Nicias the Athenian general who lost the siege of Syracuse. Executed by the Syracusans 413 BC.

Odysseus King of Ithaca who was involved in the siege of Troy.

Patroclus friend of Achilles who was killed during the siege of Troy.

Pausanias Spartan king who defeated the Persians at Plataea, d. 470 BC.

Pelopidas Theban general killed in battle 364 BC.

Philip II King of Macedon who conquered Greece. Father of Alexander the Great, d. 336 BC.

Philip V King of Macedon who was defeated by the Romans in 197 BC.

Phoenicians the occupants of ancient Lebanon in the eastern Mediterranean.

Plato Greek philosopher d. 347 BC.

Polybius 2nd-century Greek historian. Wrote a universal history covering the period from c. 250–144 BC.

Pyrrhus King of Epirus (north-west Greece) defeated the Romans at Heraclea and Asculum, 280 and 279 BC.

Scythians the name given to the barbarian races of southern Russia.

Telemachus son of Odysseus.

Themistocles Athenian politician who persuaded the Greeks to fight at Salamis, d. c. 462 BC.

Thracians the occupants of Thrace at the northern end of the Aegean.

Thucyclides 5th-century Greek historian who recorded the war between Sparta and Athens, 431–404 BC.

Vitruvius Roman architect and engineer who wrote about siege machines.

Xenophon Greek historian who wrote several books on military matters, d. c. 354 BC.

Xerxes Persian king defeated by the Greeks at Salamis 480 BC.

Places and Battles

Aegina an island between Athens and the mainland of southern Greece. It was involved in a naval war with Athens at the beginning of the 5th century.

Aegospotamoi town in the Dardanelles and scene of the Athenian naval disaster, 405 BC.

Campovalano the site of a cemetery on the eastern side of Italy from which many well preserved weapons of Greek type have been recovered.

Carthage a Phoenician city on the north coast of Africa near Tunis.

Chaeronea town of central Greece, scene of Philip II of Macedon's victory over the Greeks, 338 BC.

Corinth town at the south-west end of the isthmus that joins southern Greece to the mainland.

Delphi town of central Greece that was famous for its sanctuaries and oracle.

Dendra modern village in southern Greece where the famous Mycenaean suit of armour was found.

Epipolae plateau just north of the town of Syracuse in Sicily.

Eretria town on the west coast of the island of Euboea.

Euboea a long island on the east side of central Greece.

Gaugamela town on the east side of the Euphrates river in Iraq, scene of Alexander's third victory over Darius, 331 BC.

Granicus river in north-west Turkey, scene of Alexander's first victory over the Persians, 334 BC.

Gyphtokastro on the road between Athens and Thebes—site of an Athenian frontier fort.

Hydaspes river in north-west India, scene of Alexander's battle against the Indians, 326 BC.

Issus river near the border of Turkey and Syria. Scene of Alexander's second victory over the Persians, 333 BC.

Ithaca island on the west coast of Greece. Home of Odysseus.

Kadesh site of a great chariot battle between Egyptians and Hittites in Syria c. 1300 BC.

Kallithea village near Patrai in southern Greece. Site of a 12th century warrior's grave.

Knossos Site of the great bronze-age palace in northern Crete.

Leuctra town in central Greece. Scene of the victory of the Thebans over the Spartans, 371 BC.

Macedon area of northern Greece and southern Yugoslavia.

Mantinaea town of southern Greece. Scene of second Theban victory over the Spartans, 362 BC.

Marathon town near Athens on east coast of Greece. Scene of Athenian victory over Persians, 490 BC.

Motya Carthaginian port in western Sicily.

Mycenae town in southern Greece, the foremost town of Greece in the Mycenaean era.

Olympia town of south-west Greece famous for its sanctuaries and for the games held there. Many pieces of ancient armour have been found here.

Phalerum the old port of Athens just south of Piraeus.

Phoenicia modern Lebanon.

Piraeus the harbour of Athens.

Plataea town of central Greece. Scene of Pausanias' great victory over the Persians, 479 BC. Also scene of the Spartan siege, 429–7 BC.

Pydna site of the Macedonian defeat by the Romans 168 BC.

Raphia town in southern Israel near Gaza. Scene of battle between Syrians and Egyptians, 217 BC.

Salamis an island just off the Greek coast near Athens. Scene of the great Greek naval victory over the Persians, 480 BC.

Sparta town of southern Greece, the great opponent of Athens in the 6th and 5th centuries.

Thebes town of central Greece. The third military power of Greece, defeated Sparta in the first half of the 4th century.

Thera island in the southern Aegean Sea. It was destroyed by a volcano c. 1400 BC. Many bronze age remains have been found here.

Thermopylae village on the east coast of Greece. Scene of Leonidas' last stand against the Persians, 480 BC.

Tiryns site of a bronze-age citadel in southern Greece.

Troy a bronze-age town in north-west Turkey besieged by the Greeks, c. 1200 BC.

Tyre Phoenician town built on an island just off the coast of Lebanon. It was besieged by Alexander in 332 BC.

Index